# Foundations in Singing

SIXTH EDITION

# Foundations in Singing

*A Basic Textbook in Vocal Technique and Song Interpretation*

---

**Van A. Christy** *(deceased)*

*Professor Emeritus*
*University of California, Santa Barbara*

**John Glenn Paton**

*Professor of Voice Emeritus*
*University of Colorado, Boulder*

McGraw Hill

Boston, Massachusetts   Burr Ridge, Illinios   Dubuque, Iowa
Madison, Wisconsin   New York, New York   San Francisco, California   St. Louis, Missouri

## McGraw·Hill

*A Division of The* **McGraw·Hill** *Companies*

**Book Team**

Publisher *Rosemary Bradley*
Acquisitions Editor *Chris Freitag*
Publishing Services Coordinator *Peggy Selle*
Proofreading Coordinator *Carrie Barker*
Permissions Coordinator *LouAnn Wilson*
Production Manager *Beth Kundert*
Production/Costing Manager *Sherry Padden*
Production/Imaging and Media Development Manager *Linda Meehan Avenarius*
Visuals/Design Freelance Specialist *Mary L. Christianson*
Marketing Manager *Kirk Moen*
Copywriter *Sandy Hyde*

Basal Text *10/12 Palatino*
Display Type *Palatino Bold*
Typesetting System *Macintosh™ QuarkXPress™*
Paper Stock *50# Saturn One Offset*
Production Services *A–R Editions, Inc.*

Executive Vice President and General Manager *Bob McLaughlin*
Vice President of Business Development *Russ Domeyer*
Vice President of Production *Vickie Putman*
National Sales Manager *Phil Rudder*
National Telesales Director *John Finn*

Cover design by Wood Street Studio

Cover illustration by Andrew Powell

Copyedited by Bruce R. Owens, A–R Editions, Inc.

Proofread by Ann Kelly

# Contents

# Song Contents

# Preface

A whole generation of singers has found a solid "foundation in singing" in the earlier editions of this book. Ideas that Dr. Van A. Christy expounded at length in his two-volume *Expressive Singing* were distilled into a practical book for the vocal beginner, combined with a song anthology, in *Foundations in Singing*. Five separate editions have continued the process of keeping the book in touch with current discoveries in vocal science and current musical taste. In this sixth edition the focus remains as it has always been: to introduce new singers to the time-honored techniques of classical singing and vocal performance.

*Foundations in Singing* serves the needs of voice students in their first full year of study, whether in high school or college, whether in private lessons or in group or class instruction. By assigning readings in the textbook, the teacher can save instruction time while assuring that the student learns essential vocal vocabulary and concepts. This book uses positive, encouraging language throughout, reinforcing the teacher's role, recognizing that the student-teacher relationship remains a vital factor in successful learning.

Although the successful plan of the preceding edition remains unchanged, a number of improvements have been made:

- The text is condensed by more than ten percent without any loss of significant material.
- Page count is increased.
- The total number of songs remains at 59, but now 20 songs are printed in both high and low keys, so there is no need to buy separate volumes for high and low voices.
- Vocal exercises are provided with simple harmonizations as a guide to the accompanist.
- Recorded accompaniments are now available on audiocassettes. Although it is still ideal to have an expert accompanist in the classroom, cassettes offer an economical tool for students, both in and out of the classroom, to learn songs with strong instrumental support.

*Foundations in Singing* provides a systematic approach to vocal technique that has been validated by years of experience: attitude, posture, breathing, tone and resonance, song preparation, English diction, performance, and extending the voice. Two additional chapters on vocal physiology and music fundamentals may be introduced at various times or assigned for outside reading according to students' needs.

Thirteen songs for group singing are included here because of their usefulness for energizing a group of students, warming up their voices, and introducing musical and vocal fundamentals.

The anthology of solo songs includes an international selection of songs from folk traditions, accessible classics from four centuries, and an increased number of songs from the Broadway musical theater. All songs have been thoroughly reviewed, and primary sources from the seventeenth to the twentieth centuries have been used whenever possible.

Students who already have a foreign language background and want to use it in their singing will find songs in Italian, German, Spanish, and French. Every foreign text is translated literally on the music page where the text first appears; this translation follows normal English word order and can be extracted for use in program notes.

Appendix A provides background information about the songs, going beyond what students can normally research on their own. Background knowledge awakens students' interest and helps them relate their songs to other disciplines. The notes include interpretations of moods, unusual words in the poems, and musical sources.

Appendix B presents the complete International Phonetic Alphabet (IPA) for English.

Appendix C provides advice about singing in foreign languages. Foreign texts are retranslated word for word (not following English word order), and IPA transcriptions are also given. (Information about foreign languages is limited to whatever is necessary for the songs at hand; a complete foreign language diction course is inappropriate for the first year of vocal study.)

Appendix D is a glossary of vocal and musical terms used throughout the book.

## Acknowledgments

The task of writing a book for beginning singers has called on resources and experience from my entire life. Above all, the students who have worked with me in the past 35 years have taught me what worked and what didn't work in vocal pedagogy, and I am grateful for what I learned and for their patience with me.

Aside from the teachers mentioned in my biography, I have learned and been influenced by many others, including Laura May Titus, Dr. R. Berton Coffin, Oren Brown, Jon Peck, Mario Carta, and Jo Estill. All singers must be indebted to the National Association of Teachers of Singing for having fostered the sharing of professional knowledge to a degree that was unimaginable a generation ago.

The source notes in Appendix A refer to various libraries where I have worked; thanks go to their staff members and the benefactors and governments that support them.

Thanks to Dr. Warren Hoffer, who first recommended me to Brown & Benchmark Publishers. Helpful and specific comments about this edition have been contributed by Carol Clary-Weber, Julie Fortney, Cheryl Roach, James Stemen, and William Trabold. Elisabeth Howard suggested effective Broadway selections. Dr. René Aravena corrected the phonetic transcriptions of Spanish songs. Also, other persons have anonymously contributed their comments and suggestions through the publisher.

Finally, my thanks and love go to my wife, Joan Thompson, who supports my research and writing in every possible way and makes my books better by her perceptive comments.

With the publication of *Foundations in Singing,* plans for its next revised edition will begin immediately. Readers and users of the book are sincerely invited to send comments and suggestions to me in care of the publisher so that the next edition can be made even better.

John Glenn Paton
Los Angeles, California
Emeritus Professor of Voice, University of Colorado at Boulder
Lecturer, University of Southern California

## About the Authors

Van Ambrose Christy was born in Revere, Missouri, on Dec. 27, 1900. He received a bachelor's degree from the University of Missouri and master's and doctorate degrees from Columbia University in New York City.

Dr. Christy taught singing at the University of California at Santa Barbara for 30 years, retiring in 1968. After retirement, Prof. Christy served as a visiting professor at Brigham Young University, the University of Texas, the University of Montana, and San Francisco State University. He also conducted vocal workshops in the United States and Canada.

Christy arranged and published more than 85 choral numbers, including works for men's and women's glee clubs, and many of his arrangements were sung by the Mormon Tabernacle Choir.

In 1961 Christy achieved national recognition for his four-year course book on voice and choral teaching entitled *Expressive Singing.* This was followed by: *Expressive Singing Song Anthology* in two volumes; *Foundations in Singing*; and a collaboration with Carl Zytowski, *57 Classic Period Songs.* All of his books were published by Wm. C. Brown Company, the forerunner of Brown and Benchmark.

Christy was an avid trout fisherman and public servant. He died in 1990 at the age of 89, survived by his wife of 62 years, Hope Manchester Christy, as well as children, grandchildren, and great-grandchildren.

John Glenn Paton was born in New Castle, Pa., in 1934, the child of music teachers. He studied at the Cincinnati Conservatory of Music under Franklin Bens and Sonia Essin. After military service he studied further at the Eastman School of Music under Julius Huehn. Through both Essin and Huehn he traces his vocal lineage to Anna Schoen-René and through her to Pauline Viardot-Garcia.

After studying lieder interpretation in Stuttgart, Germany, under composer Hermann Reutter, he began to teach at the University of Wisconsin and also sang annual concert tours with Reutter as his accompanist. In 1968 he moved to the University of Colorado at Boulder, where he later received a fellowship to do a semester of research in Rome, Italy. In 1980–82 he worked for the University of Colorado in Regensburg, Germany, and had further opportunities for research in European libraries.

After moving to California in 1986 Paton taught class voice to acting students at the American Academy of Dramatic Arts, Pasadena. In 1989 he joined the faculty of the University of Southern California. He celebrated his 60th birthday by giving a solo recital, and he continues to perform occasionally.

Paton extensively revised the fifth edition of *Foundations in Singing* in 1990 and has also made instructional editions of vocal music for G. Schirmer, Leyerle Publications, and Alfred Publishing Co. His books are found in voice studios around the world.

# 1 Freedom to Sing

*Guiding questions:*     *Is singing worthwhile? Can I learn to sing with pleasure and success? How? Do I have either mental or physical blocks that will keep me from doing my best?*

WOULD you like to know how to sing well? Of course! Almost everyone would answer "Yes" to that question. Singing is such a natural part of human life that anthropologists find singing in all cultures, even the most primitive. Lullabies, play songs, love songs, hymns—they all enrich our lives and help us express our feelings. We receive great satisfaction from singing well, and society has great rewards for those who sing exceptionally well.

## Can I learn to sing?

Again, the answer is "Yes." Any person who has a normal speaking voice and can "carry a tune" (or can learn to do so) can learn to sing well and to derive enjoyment from singing. Your singing voice is a potential musical instrument, waiting for you to learn how to use it.

This idea may surprise you. Most people think of singing as an inborn talent, one that doesn't have to be learned. In fact, singing is a skill you can learn, given a capable teacher and regular practice over a period of time. Yes, talent plays a major role, but you will find that with instruction and practice your voice will improve in ways that you cannot foresee now.

If you find this hard to believe, you are not alone. Many people are afraid to sing, often because others have told them that they "can't sing." Let's look at the reasons why "fear of singing" affects some of us.

Many children live in homes where no one sings with them; they have no chance to learn the natural but complex coordination between hearing a musical tone and producing it with their voices. Many children have no music teacher in school, and classroom teachers may lack the time or the skill to lead group singing or to help those who have a hard time joining in.

Some children, both boys and girls, enjoy singing in the early grades but stop singing when they enter puberty because they feel insecure with the new physical sensations that go along with having an adult larynx. They admire good singers, but they expect the worst if they were ever to try singing. They stay silent, or perhaps they sing along with the radio when they are alone. They do not know that with instruction and a bit of courage and a short course of instruction they can start to have fun singing with and for others.

The easy availability of music on recordings and radio can even add to our "fear of singing" if we compare ourselves unrealistically with professional singers in studio recordings. That problem goes away when we find out how our listeners prefer a live performance to any music that comes through an amplifier. Recordings and radio are convenient, but they cannot replace our own self-expression. Think of singing with a group of friends around a campfire and what fun that is!

If you came through childhood and adolescence with a positive attitude about singing, count yourself lucky. You have a basis of confidence from which you can begin immediately to improve your singing and increase your knowledge about your voice. As you progress, remember to encourage others along the way; never cut down anyone who sincerely tries to sing well.

## How will I improve my singing?

Learning to sing is both a mental and a physical process: it includes both mental concepts and good muscular habits. You start out with certain vocal capabilities, including both speaking and singing. With increased awareness of how your voice works, you will use daily practice to form good vocal habits and to eliminate any vocal habits that are causing trouble. You will extend your abilities by setting step-by-step goals that allow you to experience success and to feel growing confidence. With a positive, enthusiastic approach toward learning to sing, you yourself are the most important factor in the learning process.

The second most important factor is your teacher, a person who cares about helping you to sing better and has the skill and experience to do so. If you want to know about your teacher's training and musical career, it's OK to ask.

The most basic process in voice instruction is that your teacher will *listen to you and suggest how to sing better.* This process may start at your first meeting, either with a song that you have prepared or with unrehearsed singing of a simple song like "America." Perhaps the teacher will demonstrate an exercise and ask you to sing it, too. After you have taken this first plunge, the teacher will introduce new concepts by demonstration and description with the help of readings in this book. All through your lessons, the teacher will listen for the best sounds that you can make, because it is important to notice what techniques work best for you and to use them more and more.

## Private lessons or classes?

If you are taking private voice lessons, you have two main advantages: your teacher's full attention for the length of the lesson and the privilege of moving ahead at your own pace.

If you are receiving instruction in a small group or in a voice class, you have other advantages:

- you will gain confidence from seeing that other people have fears and difficulties that are much like your own;
- you can try out new techniques in the safety of group vocalizing;
- you will trust your teacher more after seeing how other students improve with guidance;
- you will understand new concepts better through questions and discussions with your peers; and
- you will lose your qualms about singing in front of others, especially as class members give and receive mutual encouragement.

You have some responsibilities. If you are going to miss a private lesson, the teacher needs to know at least a day ahead in order to give your lesson time to someone else. If you arrive late or miss a lesson with-out advance notice, it is time lost, and you cannot expect the teacher to make it up.

If you are in a voice class, remember that you are a participating individual, not just a seat number in a lecture hall. If you arrive late or leave early, it disrupts the work that others are doing. If you miss too many classes, the process goes on for others without you. You cannot "cram" the experience of vocal growth by extra practicing before an exam.

Between meetings with your teacher, practice daily, read your assignments, and learn the assigned music. You may also be expected to learn more about singing through assigned listening and through attending musical performances.

*What will I need?*    In this book you have enough practice material and songs for your first year of vocal study.

You also need a solitary, quiet place to practice where you can make vocal experiments without worrying about who hears you or what anyone thinks. A living room with family members around is not the right place, nor is a thin-walled apartment with nearby neighbors. A practice room in a music school is ideal, or you might be able to rent a space at a local church. A practice room with a mirror will be very useful for reasons that you will learn later.

You also need some means of producing specific pitches, at best a piano or other musical instrument. A pitch pipe, available at any music store, will do, and it can be carried wherever you go. An audiocassette recorder can also be used to record the pitches you need.

An audiocassette player is an essential piece of equipment. With this book comes an audiocassette that contains piano accompaniments of all of the songs in this book. This cassette will be your personal pianist, going with you wherever you practice.

Take your cassette recorder to every class and, with your teacher's permission, use it often. The first few times you sing or vocalize in class you may be too nervous or excited to get a clear idea of how well you performed. Your recorder will let you hear again what comments were made and whether your singing actually improved as a result. A portable cassette recorder does not reproduce your voice quality perfectly, but even a poor-quality recording will tell you honestly whether you are singing on time and in tune.

# Physical freedom

Singing makes us feel good physically, provided that our bodies are healthy and we use them correctly. Right from the start we want to make sure that our bodies are physically free for singing.

Physical freedom to sing means that the muscles we need for the activity of singing are ready to work without interference from other muscles. To understand why interference occurs, we need to think about the way muscles work.

*How muscles work*    Muscle tissue characteristically has the ability to contract. When we use a muscle it receives a message through the nervous system and contracts. When we finish using that muscle it should relax but may not always do so completely. Some muscle fibers may remain tense, leaving the muscle partially contracted. If you drive on a busy freeway or carry heavy books from class to class, this kind of residual tension might give you sore shoulders or back pain. You will feel better about singing if you get rid of such tensions first.

When a muscle is activated, there may be partial activation of a neighboring muscle also because connections exist between neighboring nerves. This is a second cause of unnecessary tension. For instance, many of us have slight tensions in our speaking habits because the tiny muscles involved are so close to one another.

A third source of unnecessary tension is that, during rest, the nervous system continues to send out occasional signals to the muscles, constantly testing to be sure that the pathways for nerve impulses are open. These signals cause slight contractions of the muscles, and this is a reason our long muscles grow shorter during sleep and feel stiff when we awaken.

*Stretching*    One of the best ways to dispel tension is through *stretching* the concerned muscle groups. Gentle, patient stretching provides time for the muscle fibers to give up tensions that they no longer need. When a stretch is released, the muscle fibers return to a neutral, relaxed position. Massage is another way of allowing muscles to give up unwanted tension.

The stretching exercises given here will make you feel both more relaxed and more alive. Choose the ones that help you most. Three pieces of advice go with every exercise.

- If any exercise causes pain, stop it immediately.
- Breathe in and out normally, without holding your breath.
- A stretched muscle is in a weak position; do not shock it by a bouncing movement.

## Exercises

**1.1  Rib Stretch.** Standing with your weight on the left foot, reach up with your right arm and stretch toward the ceiling. Increase the stretch in your torso by bending your right knee. While continuing to stretch, move your arm forward and back slowly, 10–15 seconds. Relax, then repeat on the other side. Purpose: to stretch the small muscles between your ribs, the intercostals, so that you can use full lung capacity when you want to.

**1.2  Sleepyhead.** Let your head drop forward toward your chest without collapsing your shoulders, then let it fall to one side about 45 degrees. Lift your head, then let it fall forward again and to the other side about 45 degrees. Stay with each position for a few seconds. Let your head fall into position by its own weight rather than placing it. Purpose: to stretch the strong muscles that hold the head erect. (Caution: You may like to loosen your neck by rotating your head in a large circle, but that is not entirely safe for everyone.)

**1.3  Rag Doll.** Let your head drop forward, but then roll the shoulders forward and gently bend your back a little at a time, from the top down, until you have bent forward as far as you can without bending the knees. *Do not bounce* in this position, but just enjoy the stretch in your lower back. Let your head and arms hang loosely. Flex (bend) your knees a few times to increase the stretch gently. Straighten up slowly and gently. Purpose: to release back and neck tensions that may interfere with good posture and breathing.

**1.4  Neck Massage.** With the flat fingers of your right hand, massage the left side of your neck, then change sides. Enjoy the feeling. Purpose: to release tension and improve circulation in the front of the neck.

**1.5  Yawn.** Really yawn. Silently. If you don't know how to yawn at will, fake it at first and then learn to yawn at home in front of a mirror. Purpose: to stretch the back of the mouth open by lifting the soft palate and lowering the back of the tongue.

To understand the importance of yawning, swallow first. Feel the tension in your throat as the tongue rises and the soft palate closes downward against it. The swallowing muscles are very strong because we use them frequently, both awake and asleep. Yawning stretches and frees them. (Other teachers may be insulted if you yawn in class, but your voice teacher likes it!)

**1.6  Hum Slide.** Imagine a note a little higher than the pitch where you usually speak. Hum that note and let your voice slide downward. When you have done this several times comfortably, think a little higher pitch and slide down from that one. It is not important exactly what pitches you sing. Try both highs and lows that are comfortable. Purpose: to explore the whole pitch range that you can use with comfort.

**1.7  Hum Slide 5th.** To musicians, a 5th is the distance between the first and fifth notes of a scale. You can easily imagine a 5th by mentally singing the opening of "The Star-Spangled Banner": the distance between the first and third notes is the interval of a 5th. As in "hum slide," hum any pitch and slide down to another pitch a 5th lower. You may think "Oh, say!" while you hum to get the interval right. Slide down-up-down-up-down, starting on the upper note and ending on the lower one. Again, the particular pitch you sing is not important; keep changing, higher and lower. Purpose: to explore your comfortable singing range with more control of pitch.

**1.8**   **Oo Slide 5th.** Sing "Oo" softly, using the same pattern as in "hum slide 5th." Also try the syllables "You" and "Loo." Purpose: to explore your comfortable range with a quiet singing tone.

*Additional reading*    *A stimulating, fun book about mental attitudes and about solving problems in music and life is:*
*A Soprano on Her Head* by Eloise Ristad. Real People Press, Moab, UT, 1982.

*For safe ways to improve your physical fitness:*
*Stretching* by Bob Anderson. Shelter Publications (Random House), 1980.

# 2 Breath and the Body

*How should I sit or stand to sing? How do singers breathe?*

DOES just hearing the word "posture" make you stiffen up? Good posture involves more than just erectness and certainly not stiffness. Posture includes both readiness for action and the way the body is used during the action. If the body is held stiffly, then any action we do has to overcome that stiffness; if it is off balance, then we have to overcome that before the right action can take place.

## Singing posture

Good posture for singing means using the body in a balanced way so that our breathing muscles work easily and we produce the sound we want without any physical interference.

Experienced performers can sing in almost any position, even lying down. Performers in musical theater must be able to sing while dancing, and in India and many other countries singers sit down to perform. However, while we are discovering and freeing our voices, an erect posture gives us the best start. Any poor postural habits must first be corrected before proper breath control can be established.

Here are some characteristics of good singing posture:

- Feet: Place your heels a few inches apart with your toes turned out slightly. Balance your weight evenly, with one foot a little forward, and keep both feet on the floor. The position in Figure 2.1a gives you a firm basis yet allows you to move in any direction with minimal effort. If your feet are too close together, as in Figure 2.1b, your posture looks stiff or you may weave around.

**Figure 2.1**

- Legs: Straight, but not locked rigidly at the knees.
- Torso: Level, both at hip height and at shoulder height. The abdominal muscles in the front and the spinal column in the back work together to support and straighten the torso.

    Avoid curving your back too far inward. A swaybacked position weakens the spine and makes it prone to injury. Because this posture throws the viscera (the "innards") too far forward, the abdominal muscles are stretched into a weakened state and cannot give us the flexible breath control we need.

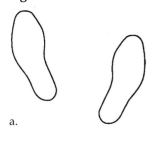

a.

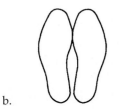

b.

- Shoulders: Level. Let them relax downward and back.

    Some of us hunch up our shoulders because of fear or insecurity, for instance, before a difficult note. This fear reflex makes our listeners uncomfortable, too. Relaxing our shoulders counteracts the reflex and improves our confidence. On the other hand, if we let our shoulders slouch forward, wanting to look casual and easygoing, we may just look lazy or lacking in confidence.

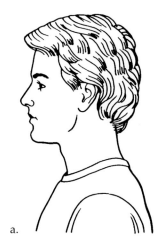  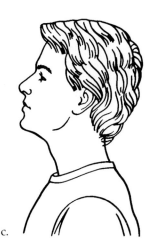

a.            b.            c.

**Figure 2.2**

- Neck and Head: Let them rise effortlessly toward the ceiling.

  Imagine that a puppeteer is lifting you from above by a hook set into your head, directly over and between your ears. Let your head remain level so that your eyes look straight ahead, neither down nor up (Figure 2.2a).

  Avoid slouching, with your head forward of your center of gravity (Figure 2.2b), and avoid tilting your head up (Figure 2.2c). These common faults cause many problems, as we will see.

*Head alignment*

Knowing that a person's spine runs up the back, we might think that the spine connects to the back of the head. If this were so, the weight of the head (usually more than 11 pounds) would be held in front of the spine, requiring muscular energy to hold it up.

In fact, the spine curves sharply inward to a point near the middle of the neck. We cannot feel the topmost vertebra, but it slants forward and has two small surfaces on which the skull rests. The point of contact is between our ears, close behind the back wall of the throat (Figure 2.3). When the head balances correctly on the spine, it takes little or no muscular effort to stay aligned.

Clearly, if the spine slumps forward and the weight of the head is constantly in front of the body's center of gravity, the neck muscles have to work to keep the head from falling forward. As pointed out in chapter 1, tension can spread from those muscles to the front of the neck and interfere with singing.

A slouched posture also stretches the muscles at the front of the neck somewhat, and they become less free to do what we want.

Avoid stretching your neck to reach for high notes. Children do so because their soft voice boxes need the pull of external muscles, but adults do not need to stretch their necks.

# Learn to breathe

We have been breathing at an average of twenty times per minute all our lives, breathing faster when we exercise and using our breath to speak and shout all we want. Even so, singing makes special demands on our breath.

- Singing a long musical phrase depends on both the volume of air in our lungs and on our ability to release air slowly and steadily.

- Singing louder and softer and singing with expression and variety depend on our ability to vary the rate of airflow.

- Musical rhythm often requires us to breathe in quickly between phrases.

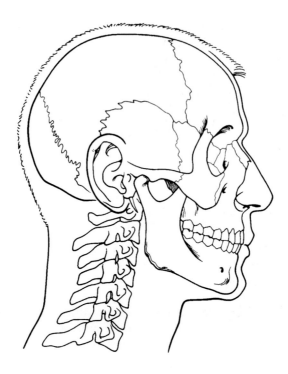

We want to release breath energy at a precisely controlled rate for a desired length of time and to renew the energy quickly. This sums up what we mean by *breath control*. If "control" has a negative meaning for you, you can use a more positive phrase: *breath management.*

To manage our breath efficiently we use the parts of the body that combine flexibility and muscular strength, especially the area of the lower ribs and the abdominal wall. Although many muscle groups are involved, the next section attempts to describe their action as simply as possible.

*The breathing mechanism*

Air fills the lungs, two spongy sacks that are passive and nonmuscular. The lungs are contained in the bony cage of the ribs (Figure 2.4), and when the rib cage expands, air rushes in to fill the lungs automatically.

Individual ribs, being bone, do not stretch or bend. The rib cage as a whole is flexible because the bones are held together by flexible tissues. The ribs move somewhat like curved bucket handles, fanning out wider when they are lifted by the chest and back muscles.

In back, all twelve ribs on each side are attached to the spine. In front, the seven highest ribs are attached to the breastbone (sternum). They have only a small range of motion and a well-trained singer keeps them lifted at all times.

The next three ribs move more freely; they are attached to one another by cartilage, but are not attached to the breastbone. The two lowest ribs are attached only to the spine.

All of the lower ribs rise and move outward to increase the space in the lungs and to let air in. They can also be lowered and narrowed to push air out. This way of releasing the breath involves moving rigid and rather heavy bones and so does not result in as much ease and precision of movement as we need.

A better way of releasing the breath is by using the most flexible part of the rib cage, a complex muscle called the *diaphragm* (Greek: partition). The diaphragm closes the bottom of the breath chamber, the *thorax,* and separates it from the digestive organs below. The diaphragm is attached at its edges to the

**Figure 2.4**
*The rib cage, viewed from slightly above and to the right of center. Intercostal muscles are left out so that the spine can be seen between the ribs. Observe that ribs 1–7 meet the sternum, whereas ribs 8–10 are each attached in succession to the next rib above. Ribs 11 and 12 are attached only to the spine.*

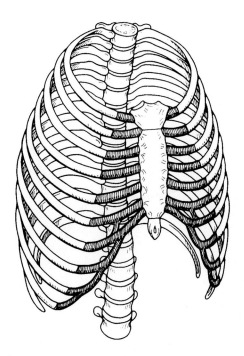

spine, the sternum, and the lowest ribs. The "food pipe" (esophagus) and blood vessels pass through openings in the diaphragm to reach the lower body.

When the diaphragm relaxes, it has the shape of two domes, one under each lung (shown by the heavy black line in Figure 2.5). When the diaphragm contracts, its domelike curves flatten downward, creating more space in the chest cavity and allowing air to rush in (shown by the dotted line in Figure 2.5). This action pushes down on viscera below and causes the abdominal wall to move outward.

When people speak of "breathing from the diaphragm" and pat their tummies, they are really talking about the upper part of the abdominal wall, the *epigastrium*, which moves outward when the diaphragm lowers. The diaphragm itself is inside the body, where it is neither seen nor felt. It has no proprioceptors, the nerves that report sensations of pain or position to the brain.

*Breath support*

As we sing, the muscles at the front and sides of the epigastrium and/or the ribs (the *costal* area) must move in. The costal and epigastrium muscles can work together to empty the lungs very quickly, much too quickly for singing. We slow down the process and control the airflow by using opposing muscles, or antagonists. We purposely keep the ribs expanded for as long as possible while the diaphragm continues the downward push that brought the air in.

The balanced use of these muscles is called "costal-epigastrium breathing." It happens simply as a result of our decision to breathe out slowly, even though we cannot control the diaphragm consciously.

To understand the opposition (antagonism) of the breathing muscles, put one hand on top of the other with the palms together and push them against each other. One hand pushes down like the diaphragm while the other pushes up like the upward and inward pull of the abdominal wall. The result is a slow movement that can be precisely controlled.

When we have this slow, steady movement combined with a well-produced tone, we say that we have "breath support" or that the tone is well "supported."

**Chapter 2**

**Figure 2.5**

*The position of the lungs in the rib cage. The dark line shows the relaxed position of the diaphragm, and the dotted line shows the contracted position.*

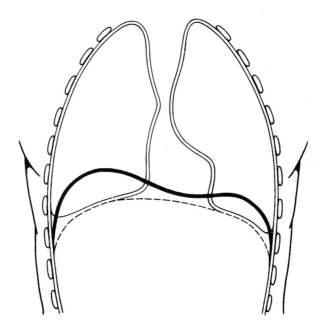

*Phases of breath action*

In daily life we think of breath in two phases: in and out. For singing we can consider four phases: inhalation, turnaround, exhalation, and recovery.

1. *Inhalation* is taken through both the mouth and the nose, or through the nose only if time allows. With the ribs already lifted and widened, you sense the throat as open and relaxed. Sense the body as opening deeply when the diaphragm descends and the abdominals relax. Inhale positively and deeply, but don't "cram" the lungs with air. Imagine the coming note so that you will be ready with the right pitch and the right vowel or consonant. Let in enough air to sing the coming phrase, plus a little reserve.

2. *Turnaround* is a split second when your diaphragm has reached its lowest point and the abdominals begin to resist it. Let your vocal cords remain open. Your vocal instrument is ready to sing.

3. *Exhalation* produces the tone. Let a gentle movement of your abdominals, working slowly against the resistance of the diaphragm, slightly compress your air supply; it rises through the voice box, creating the tone.
   Abdominal action alone is enough for a short phrase. The end of a longer phrase may also require the ribs to move inward. If the rib cage collapses, the results are muscular tension and a poor sound.

4. *Recovery* is the opposite of the turnaround phase: a moment of relaxation for the muscles. Let the abdomen relax outward (without losing your posture). Let the ribs regain their wide position. If you have time to rest, breathe normally; if the music goes on quickly, you can reverse the flow of air as quickly as you did in the turnaround phase.

Some experts speak of all four phases as parts of one smoothly continuous cycle. You can visualize it as a circular movement or as the lapping of waves on the shore of the ocean.

*Theories of breath support*

All singers use the process described above, but individual singers and teachers explain the process in different ways and emphasize different parts of it in their practicing and singing. The result is that one can hear and read many theories about breath support.

Some singers stress sensations of downward and outward pushing, while others think in terms of more relaxed, flowing movements. Some singers concentrate on the epigastrium area, while others use the whole abdominal muscle wall as a single unit. Others say that the "secret" of support lies in the back muscles, which certainly help out by holding the ribs up. Still others believe that the whole process will occur automatically if our mental concepts of tone are correct. Regarding such a complex musculature, it is no wonder that artists use it in a variety of ways.

In action, breath support means keeping the tone flowing evenly, freely, and firmly. We may find that at times we need to concentrate on holding the breath back, while at other times we need to remind ourselves not to block the outward flow.

Breath control also involves tone control and is dependent for success on efficient resonance. Breath management and good tone develop together; both must be mastered over an extended period.

## Interaction between posture and breath action

You have a foundation for good breath action if

1. the spine feels flexibly stretched, lifted by the buoyancy of the head;
2. the chest remains comfortably high and quiet during singing, not rigidly high, as when a soldier stands at attention; and
3. the ribs widen by action of the back muscles before inhalation starts. If this is not done, you will probably lift the chest to inhale, starting a motion that pumps the chest up on every inhalation and collapses it on every exhalation.

### Upside-down breathing

Toddlers breathe correctly, but by adulthood many of us have lost the knack. If you breathe by lifting your chest and pulling in your abdomen, as many people do, then you are not really getting a "deep breath" but a high, tense breath. You are "filling up" instead of "breathing deep."

Upside-down breathing causes at least three problems:

1. Your pulled-in abdominal muscles are stiff before you start to sing, so they cannot help move the air out.
2. When you breathe out, your rib cage falls, affecting your posture and causing tension in the neck muscles.
3. Because the weight of your ribs is providing some of the air compression, you have less resilience than if the lower muscles were doing the work.

You need to retrain your breathing reflexes, a process that may take several days or several weeks. Start out by relaxing the abdominal muscles during inhalation.

### Bodybuilding

The breathing exercises that follow will benefit anyone who is below normal in physical vitality or weak in chest development.

Bodybuilding, however, is not our goal; most normally active persons are strong enough for voice study. Some very muscular students find it hard to relax their neck and abdomen muscles enough to sing freely. Exercise to invigorate and strengthen your body, not to exhaust it.

Students sometimes wonder out loud whether breathing exercises will thicken their waistlines. Quite the opposite! Good abdominal muscles are essential to a good figure. Incidentally, they also support the back muscles and help us avoid back pains.

**Figure 2.6**

**Exercises**

Repeat the stretching exercises from chapter 1, and keep them as part of your daily warm-up. Try out the sensation of letting your head float toward the ceiling, with your spine dangling from your head and the shoulders and arms relaxed. Feel how pleasant this is, and remind yourself of it often. Add the following exercises.

2.1   **Shoulder Roll.** In a circular motion, let both shoulders move back, up, forward and down. Make at least four circles; then at least four circles in the opposite direction. End with the shoulders relaxed and low. Purpose: to release any tensions that are stiffening the shoulder muscles.

    Notice that you can do this exercise with the chest either lifted or collapsed. Naturally, a lifted position is better, but this exercise shows that the shoulders are independent from the chest position and do not hold the chest up.

2.2   **Abdominal Action.** Standing erect, raise both arms toward the ceiling so that the rib cage rises. Briefly tense the abdominals and move them in while you make the consonant sound "sh." Then relax the abdominals and let them move out while air comes into the lungs. Do this in a rhythm, alternating one second of sound with one second of silence. Purpose: to sense the bellowslike action of the abdominals and to overcome any stiffness in this area. Take turns with a partner (as in Figure 2.6), who checks whether the abdominals are moving in the right direction.

2.3   **Rib-widening.** Place your fists against your sides and feel the width of your rib cage. Exhale fully so that your rib cage is as narrow as possible. Let your ribs relax and widen and then consciously spread them as wide as possible. Your ribs should push your fists outward one inch or more on

**Figure 2.7**

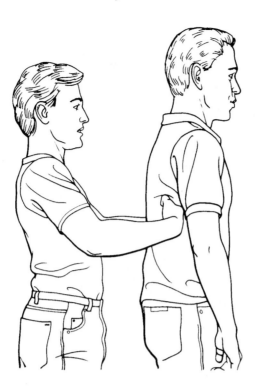

each side. Hold for about four seconds and then relax. Purpose: to develop awareness of the potential expansion of the rib cage. Let your partner check your rib expansion (as in Figure 2.7).

During this exercise you are probably using rib breathing only. That's why this exercise is for discovery, not for daily drill. Repeat it only when you need a reminder of your vital capacity.

**2.4   Full Breath Action.** Phase 1: While you take a slow, deep inhalation through the nose, with your mouth open but your jaw relaxed, raise your arms steadily from your sides, palms down, on a slow count of 1–2–3–4, until your palms meet over your head (as in Figure 2.8). Phase 2: Keep your arms up for a slow count of 1–2–3–4. At this point the ribs have their maximum expansion, the diaphragm has lowered, and the abdominals have relaxed outward. Phase 3: Let your arms come down while you exhale on a hissing "sh" or "ss" to a slow count of 1–2–3–4. Keep the chest lifted and ribs expanded until the abdominals have finished their lift inward against the diaphragm. Purpose: to build a habit of sustaining an open rib cage and free, vital breathing with the muscles around the waistline. Phase 4: Rest for a count of 1–2–3–4 with an erect posture.

Notice that when you repeat the exercise in a continuous rhythm, the ribs stay expanded with the help of the back muscles. Once lifted and expanded by the first arm lift, the ribs do not need to be lifted again; the arm movement simply reminds us of their position and helps us correct any temporary slump. Practice this daily until your back muscles can sustain a singing posture for several minutes at a time.

Variations:

a.   Increase the exhalation count to 6 or 8. Keep the inhalation count at 4 or reduce it to 2.

b.   Change the "ss" to "zz" or "vv" so that the vocal cords are used for the sound.

**Figure 2.8**

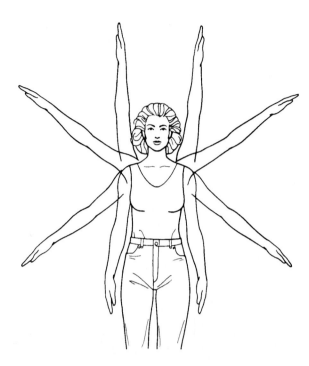

    c.    Open your mouth and speak the syllable "huh," letting it last as long as the inhalation.

    d.    Eventually, omit the arm action when you no longer need constant reminders of expansion.

*Voice exercises*

Repeat all of the exercises from chapter 1; they are part of your daily warm-up. Do them with awareness of the breath action you learned in this chapter.

**2.5**    **Panting.** Place the fingertips on the stomach wall in the epigastrium area just below the breastbone. With the chest comfortably high, quickly inhale a vigorous breath (the fingertips move outward). Release the breath suddenly, speaking a "sh" sound. Repeat vigorously and rhythmically in a series of panting pulsations. Purpose: to induce a sensation of vigorous breath muscle action and quick inhalation.

**2.6**    **Bubble Slide.** Through gently closed lips, blow enough air to make your lips vibrate, as if you were blowing bubbles under water or imitating the sound of a motorcycle. Add vocal tone to make a "bubble slide" like the "hum slide" you learned in chapter 1. (Recall the relaxed, low position of the jaw after yawning; keep the feeling of a loose jaw at all times.) Purpose: to produce tone with a vigorous and steady breath flow through a comfortable pitch range while eliminating tension from the lips.
Variations:

    a.    **Bubble Slide 5th.** Practice this on the same musical interval as "hum slide 5th." (Do you remember "Oh, say"?)

    b.    **Tongue Roll Slide.** Do the action of "rolling an rr" with no vocal tone at first, then add tone to make a slide. Purpose: to produce tone with a vigorous and steady breath flow while eliminating tension in the tongue.

    If you have trouble producing a "tongue roll," you are not alone. About ten percent of English-speaking people have this problem. If you have trouble with both the "bubble" and the "tongue roll," sing on a soft "oo" in class and keep experimenting with them outside of class.

**2.7** **Starter.** Hum the following rhythm on any comfortable pitch. Use "panting" breath action, but let it be more gentle. Purpose: to combine agile breath muscle action with accurate attacks on a single pitch, preparing for the quick breaths often needed in songs.

In all exercises, the lower notes are for the lower voices in a voice class.

Variations: Sing the syllables "uh" and "ee."

**2.8** **Stepper.** Hum the following pattern, starting on any comfortable pitch. Purpose: to combine agile breath muscle action with the accurate attacks on changing pitches.

Variations: Sing the syllables "uh" and "ee."

**2.9** **Slow Stepper.** Hum the following pattern, starting on any comfortable pitch. Purpose: same as "Stepper."

Variations: Sing the syllables "uh" and "ee."

*A closing thought*

When you sing songs, your mind will be on the words and notes, not on your breathing. The purpose of practicing at this stage is to make correct breathing action so natural to you that it will continue automatically even when you are not thinking about it. This does not happen overnight. You may need a lot of practice before correct breath action will continue through a whole phrase or a whole song. In the meantime, remind yourself often to use correct breath action at least for the starts of phrases.

*Additional reading*

*A practical, illustrated book of exercises that will help you stand, sit, and move more efficiently and gracefully:*
*The Alexander Technique* by Sarah Barker. Bantam Books, 1978.

*A scientifically sound, detailed, but clear description of the physiology of singing, including photographs of a dissected diaphragm and other vocal organs:*
*Dynamics of the Singing Voice* by Meribeth Bunch Third edition. Springer-Verlag, 1995.

# 3 Free Tone

**Guiding questions:** *How can I think and talk about vocal tone? How should I start a tone? Stop a tone?*

EACH of us has an individual voice quality unlike anyone else's because of the unique characteristics of each individual vocal instrument. In addition to a unique personal sound, we can also make many choices about ways of using our voices. When we produce tonal qualities we like, we can choose to use them more often and eliminate qualities we do not like. In this chapter we will consider various kinds of tone quality, as well as how to start and stop tones.

## Tone quality

Think of a voice you like to hear. What words describe the way that voice sounds?

Too often, people answer this question with judgmental words like "pretty" or "beautiful" and stop there. We need a wider vocabulary of words that describe tones we like and don't like; it will help us make decisions about how to improve our own voices.

### Descriptive words

Here are some words, arranged in contrasting pairs, that voice teachers sometimes use to describe voices. These words are not scientific terms, and not everyone would agree on what they mean, but all of them relate to vocal *technique*.

- agile—stiff
- breathy—clear
- even—uneven
- lyric—dramatic
- crooning—supported
- forced—free

- dull—resonant
- nasal—throaty
- somber—bright
- harsh—mellow
- strong—weak

Here are other, more subjective words that describe how a voice affects our emotions: timid, bold, irritating, boring, soothing, warm, velvety, brassy, authoritative, ingratiating, shrill.

Can you think of other words that describe the effect of individuals' voices on you? How would you like other people to describe the effect of your voice? Consider what these words mean to you. Do they describe some recorded voices you know? Which words describe your singing right now?

### Vocal acoustics

The science of *acoustics* explains differences in tone quality in terms of the *overtones* that accompany musical tones. Briefly, every vocal tone consists of a basic pitch, the *fundamental*, and also numerous vibrations at higher pitches (overtones) going on simultaneously. Normally, you are not aware of hearing overtones, but you perceive them in terms of tone colors.

If you sing one pitch while changing the vowel from "ah" to "ee," the fundamental does not change, but the overtones do; you are strengthening some overtones and weakening others. The change takes place automatically in response to your mental image of the sound you want to make. This easy, normal process reveals a basic principle: *You will change and develop your vocal quality by imagining the sounds you want.* Any vocal instrument has some limitations, of course, but most of us have far more possibilities than we imagine.

*Tonal goals*

What are some characteristics of a "good" voice, one that we like to hear?

1. **Audibility.** We want to hear a voice easily in a fair-sized room without a microphone. Anyone can meet this goal. If you practice applying energy to your voice and removing physical tensions, your voice will develop enough carrying power to sing in public. Good teachers agree that a strong tone is a by-product of good vocal habits, not a goal in itself.

2. **Resonance.** A quality of "ring" in the voice results from strong overtones, particularly certain ones at a very high pitch that affect the human ear pleasantly. Even a low male voice requires these high overtones, up around 2,800–3,200 Hertz (vibrations per second). A voice without them seems dull, lacking in beauty and carrying power. Again, any healthy voice can develop enough "ring" for good singing.

3. **Clarity.** We prefer a clear tone with no extra noises (for instance, breathiness) that interfere with the overtones.

4. **Intelligibility.** This refers to clarity of consonant and vowel formation. Anyone who really cares about communicating with an audience can achieve this with intelligent hard work.

5. **Pure intonation.** Good musicianship requires an ability to start, continue, and stop a tone on pitch without sliding up or down unintentionally. (If you suspect you might be tone-deaf, look up this topic in chapter 12.)

6. **Dynamic variety.** Musical expression requires an ability to sing softer and louder, with smooth changes from one level to another.

7. **Timbral variety.** Dramatic expression requires an ability to change vocal tone-color (timbre), with "bright" tones (stronger high partials) and "dark" tones (weaker high partials) and other qualities produced in response to your imagination and feelings.

8. **Vibrato.** A well-produced voice is capable of a regular, periodic pitch oscillation above and below a basic pitch. More is said about vibrato later in this chapter.

9. **Range.** Most songs require more than an octave (8 scale tones). "The Star-Spangled Banner" requires a twelfth (12 scale tones). A professional singer is expected to sing at least two octaves (15 scale tones) with comfort and good quality, not counting some weaker tones below and above the range that is usable in public performance. In fact, every healthy voice has a range of more than two octaves, needing only the skill and practice to make those tones usable. Range, like loudness, is a by-product of good vocal habits, not a goal in itself.

10. **Ease/freedom.** Good singing takes both mental and physical effort, but the audience doesn't want to know about that. The singer should look, as well as sound, comfortable.

These are characteristics of a good voice. Which ones do you already have to a satisfactory degree? Do any of these characteristics seem difficult to develop? Don't worry. Chances are that you can develop all of them in time.

Does this mean that anyone can become a great singer? No, of course not. Anyone can swing a baseball bat, but not everyone can play in the major leagues. A professional singer possesses all of the basic resources listed above and uses them with superior skill, refinement, and imagination.

We can hardly begin to list what goes into a major singing career: years of study, strong musical skills, superior health, vivid personality, artistic creativity, dramatic flair, and much more. Business sense, unflagging ambition, ability to choose the right teachers, coaches, agents, and, yes, money are also ingredients in most singing careers. Furthermore, not everyone who could have a singing career wants one enough to live the demanding life of a performer.

But if you are not going to be a professional singer, is your voice worth developing? Yes, definitely. Set your own goals and decide what priority singing has in your life. Your goal may be to sing in a barbershop chorus, to entertain your friends, to sing at worship services, or to participate in a community chorus or theater. These are all realizable goals. Between choral singing and solo stardom there is an infinite number of possibilities for artistic self-expression and satisfaction. With time, work, training, and imagination you may go much further than you imagine right now.

## What the vocal cords do

Moving air causes a tone by vibrating the vocal cords. Chapter 11 describes the vocal cords in some detail, but at this point you need to know three things about them.

1. The vocal cords can be brought together over the windpipe, closing it so tightly that no air can enter or leave the lungs.

2. They are drawn apart when we breathe in and out normally, allowing air to pass between them (as in Figure 11.2 on page 68).

3. They come together during singing but loosely enough so that air can still escape between them and make them vibrate. Tiny puffs of air coming through the cords cause the sound waves that resonate in the throat and mouth to make tone.

## Attack and release

The start of a musical tone is commonly called the *attack*. A good tone can only come from a good attack. If an attack is shaky or out of tune, the whole phrase is likely to go out of tune. Likewise, a tone quality that is harsh and tense on the attack is likely to remain tense to the end of the phrase. Aim for a free, clear, effortless tone on the attack.

The first and most important advice regarding the attack is to imagine the tone—the pitch, quality, and dynamic level—before you sing it. A good attack starts with a mental impulse put into action by the breath, not by the throat.

*Release* is the ending of a musical tone. Again, a correct release results from a mental decision to stop or reverse the flow of breath. When we sing one phrase after another, the release of one phrase reverses the air flow to prepare for the next phrase.

### Three methods of attack

The facts given above about the vocal cords help us understand the three methods of attack: *glottal*, breathy, and clean.

1. *Glottal attack* occurs when the vocal cords are held closed and air pressure pushes them apart to start the tone. If the resulting sound is explosive and coughlike, it can damage the vocal cords.

2. *Breathy attack* occurs when air passes between the vocal cords before they meet and begin vibrating. This happens every time we say the consonant

"h." Breathy attack is preferable to glottal attack, but it often leads to breathiness in the tone.

3.   *Clean attack* occurs when the movement of air and the closure of the vocal cords are practically simultaneous. Fortunately, the body coordinates this delicate adjustment automatically if we have a clear mental concept of the desired tone.

One important function of the vocal cords is to close off the windpipe when it is necessary to pressurize the air in the lungs. Many people do this when exerting the upper body, as in lifting a heavy weight or chopping wood. High pressure on the vocal cords and friction between them can cause wear and tear, just as when you cough too much. For this reason you should learn to exercise without holding your breath. (Weightlifters have a good slogan: "Blow the weight up.")

Similarly, some people habitually speak with glottal stops, closing the vocal cords before every word that begins with a vowel and blowing the cords open with a little coughing sound. This abuses the vocal cords, as all speech therapists agree.

*Three methods of release*

Because of the way the vocal cords work, there are three methods of releasing a tone, just as there are three methods of attack.

1.   *Stopped release.* The vocal cords close together tightly, ending the tone but also preventing any intake of breath. This causes unnecessary friction and vocal damage, just as a glottal attack does.

2.   *Breathy release.* The vocal cords separate, correctly ending the tone, but extra air continues to flow. This delays our preparation to continue singing and perhaps makes an unwanted noise.

3.   *Clean release.* The diaphragm drops, the vocal cords separate, and air flows into the lungs simultaneously.

Obviously, the only desirable release is the "clean" one, in which the ending of one tone simultaneously begins the preparation for the next.

*Resonance*

If we could hear a vocal sound that comes directly from the vocal cords, we would find it dull and unattractive. The sound waves that come from the vocal cords gain strength and quality from bouncing back and forth in the resonators, which are the throat, mouth, and other spaces of the neck and head. Resonators are partially enclosed spaces within which sound waves reinforce themselves and grow stronger.

A resonant tone can be felt as vibrations in the important resonators. When you hear a tone you like, notice not only the sound of it but also how the vibrations feel in your mouth, throat, and head. This will help you produce the same tone again.

*Vibrato*

A student who was searching for words asked me, "What do you call it when a voice kind of waves up and down and it's nice?" Answer: *Vibrato*, one of the qualities we listen for in a voice, whether we realize it or not. When we hear a vibrato, we feel that a voice is free and relaxed, warm and expressive. Vibrato is such a natural part of a freely produced voice that we are likely to think that a voice without it is "no good."

Some singers have vibrato from childhood and are never without it. They may be asked to eliminate or reduce their vibrato in some styles of choral music. Other singers could use vibrato but inhibit it. The following are some reasons I have heard:

"Someone said that if I try to use vibrato it will be unnatural; I should wait until I'm older and it will come naturally." False: The vibrato you have in your teens is yours. Use it with pride.

"The choir director said my vibrato made my voice stick out." Translation: One mature voice among other immature voices caused a problem that the director didn't have time to solve. It would be better to improve the weaker voices than to stifle the one good voice.

"I don't want my voice to sound 'operatic' and affected." Don't worry, you won't go overboard. Try singing with vibrato and you will find that your friends like it.

With an attitude change, such students sometimes begin to use vibrato immediately. All they need is to give themselves permission.

Figure 3.1 shows in a simplified way how a tone with vibrato rises above and falls below the pitch at a rate of six or seven cycles per second. The voice may rise and fall as much as a quarter tone above and below the basic pitch. At the same time, the volume and tone quality also vary.

**Figure 3.1**

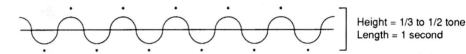

Height = 1/3 to 1/2 tone
Length = 1 second

As with the other characteristics of a good voice, almost everyone can develop a pleasing vibrato. (Some individuals have difficulty recognizing vibrato, as music psychologists have found. Even some accomplished singers who have a normal vibrato are unable to say whether they have one or not.) If you have never used vibrato in your voice, it may take a while before you achieve the right balance of energy and relaxation to allow vibrato to occur spontaneously. If you sing a tone with vibrato, take notice of it and encourage it to reappear.

Different singing styles use vibrato differently; some country singers seldom use it, whereas some gospel and blues singers use more than a half-tone. Jazz stylists, particularly, add and subtract vibrato at will as part of their expressive technique.

Sometimes we hear a vibrato that is too wide, too fast, or too slow or one that pulses loud and soft like a bleat. We use the word *tremolo* to describe any such unpleasant vibratos. Tremolos can usually be corrected by improving breath support and learning the right balance of vitality and relaxation in singing.

## How to vocalize

Repeat the exercises from chapters 1 and 2. Each chapter adds to your repertoire of exercises that help you get ready to sing every day, whether or not you feel inspired. Especially, repeat "abdominal action," "rib-widening," and "full breath action" until you feel confident that you breathe correctly for singing at any time, at will. Repeat the voice exercises with added awareness of attack and release.

Here is some advice to help you get your best tone in the next exercises.

1.  Use a hummed consonant, *n* or *m*, to prepare a resonant intensity for the tone.

2.  Test for harmful glottal attacks. Stop both ears with your fingers, then hum a tone in easy range. If there is a glottal attack, you will hear and feel the click or coughlike attack. To change this habit, temporarily start each tone with a "silent h," a little breath that escapes ahead of the tone. You can easily drop this habit when you no longer need it.

3.  Endeavor to carry the humming intensity of *n* or *m* into *Uh*, a neutral vowel that is formed with a uniformly open vocal passage. Think of *Uh* as a free and ringing tone (Up!), never muffled (Dull!) in tonal character.

4.  Use *Uh*, with its free, open-throated feeling, as the basis for other vowels. Transitions from *n* to *Uh* to *Oh* or *Ee* should be smooth and flowing, with no feeling of changing resonance space.

**5.**    Use a vital and comfortable tone with a medium dynamic level, either medium loud (mf) or medium soft (mp).

*What pitch to sing*    Explore your voice, trying many different pitches—medium, low, and high. Exercises can begin on any pitch that is comfortable in your range.

Start each exercise somewhat above your normal speaking pitch. Sing it twice or more, noticing how it improves with repetition; then transpose it downward several times to lower keys. Repeat the exercise on a somewhat higher starting pitch and again move downward several times. Repeat a key whenever you feel you can improve the tone. Start over again in a higher key, if you can do so without a sense of reaching or straining.

This is a strategy for exploring your higher range with ease. "Take what the voice gives you," as voice teacher Oren Brown expresses it, rather than force the voice to sing a wider range.

# Exercises

The first new exercises, 3.1 through 3.3, use a clean attack as we usually use it in normal *legato* singing. Purpose: to produce a free, efficient, uniform tone with clean attack and release in various musical situations.

**3.1    Hummer.**                                  **3.2    Down Five.**

**3.3    Singles.**

**3.4    Tune-up.** Sing the quick syllables lightly, pronouncing *m*'s and *n*'s quickly. Keep the jaw out of action as much as possible. In voice classes, sing in two parts. Purpose: to prepare for sustaining long tones with continued vitality and freshness.

3.5 **Yummies.** The glide sound "Y" brightens the tone. Purpose: to develop a relaxed, resonant tone with a sense of high, forward resonance. Suggestion: in voice class sing this in canon, with half of the voices beginning on beat three.

Yum-my, yum-my, yum-my, yum-my, yum!    Yum-my, yum-my, yum-my, yum-my, yum!

Yum-my, yum-my, yum-my, yum-my, yum!    Yum-my, yum-my, yum-my, yum-my, yum!

*Additional listening*

*Learn about different kinds of tone quality by listening to recordings of singing styles that are unfamiliar to you. Some examples might be Italian opera, Native American songs, Beijing opera, Renaissance music using a countertenor voice, Wagnerian opera, music from India, 1930s jazz and blues, and various pop styles. Examples should be available in any public library listening area.*

# 4 Changing Resonances in Your Voice

*Guiding questions:* *Why do the upper notes of my voice sound and feel different from the lower notes? What kinds of voices are there, and what kind do I have? How can I make my voice more resonant?*

HAVE you noticed that some parts of your voice feel different from others? Can you sing some notes in more than one way? Untrained singers often feel uncomfortable because some notes of their voices are weaker than other notes. Let's learn about them and find out how to work with them.

## Chest or head?

Try this experiment: place your hands on your ribs and sing a strong tone on a fairly low pitch. What do you feel? You probably feel vibrations in your bones. Now keep your hands on your ribs and sing a high, light note. Do you still feel the vibrations? Probably not. Now start on a high note and let the pitch slide downward. As the pitch goes down, you will reach a pitch where you feel the ribs begin to vibrate again.

Centuries ago singers noticed these sensations. Not knowing about the vocal cords, they thought that certain tones originated in the chest and others in the head. This is not true—chest vibration is simply a response to tone, a sympathetic vibration. However, many singers still speak of chest voice and head voice because of the sensations that accompany our low and high registers.

Luckily, our voices have many qualities available, not just two. When we imagine tones, our vocal cords adjust themselves subtly, changing in length, in thickness, in shape, and in the amount of contact between them. Chest voice and head voice don't just change like the flick of a switch. Good singers continually mix and blend their tones when they decide how loud or soft to sing and what quality to use. They do this simply by imagining the tone quality they want to use.

Our ideal goal in classical singing is to have all notes equal in quality and strength. This could be described as a voice with one *register*, meaning that the highest and lowest notes and all the notes in between sound alike. Some voice teachers speak of a one-register voice that is either a rare gift of nature or the result of years of training. Others think that a one-register voice is an illusion that a skillful singer creates.

Whatever one may think about one register, most students are well aware of unequal tones in their voices. A majority of singers are aware of three registers:

1. head or light mechanism;
2. medium or blended mechanism; and
3. chest or heavy mechanism.

Three registers were recognized in the 1840s by Manuel Garcia II, the first person who ever used a dental mirror to observe the vocal cords during singing.

In *Hints on Singing* he offered this classic definition: "A register is a series of consecutive homogeneous sounds produced by one mechanism. . . ."

Other theories of registers also have followers. Dr. R. Berton Coffin agreed that vocal cords act differently in various registers, but he showed that there are also acoustical distinctions between them. Coffin identified eleven registers, of which the lowest ones are used only by basses and the highest ones only by sopranos.

These differing theories still have some common ground:

1. Men do most of their singing in the chest voice, blending to the medium and head for their higher notes.

2. Women do most of their singing in the head voice, blending to medium and chest for their lower notes.

3. The registers overlap a great deal, allowing us to make choices according to the tone quality and loudness desired.

*Your choice*

Which register do you like to use when you sing? Which is your strongest?

Let's start by thinking about your speaking voice. Is it high or low? Our modern culture prefers low speaking voices. Parents admonish children to keep their voices down. Girls may or may not realize that their voices drop by four or five notes during puberty, but they definitely feel more grown up when their voices lose the squeakiness of childhood. When adolescent boys' voices drop an octave or more, their friends and family praise them for sounding like men. Many of us, both female and male, respond to positive responses from the people around us by lowering our speaking pitch, sometimes even more than is natural.

You can test the pitch of your own speaking voice (perhaps with your teacher's help). Speak a syllable that you can hold onto easily and strike a note on the piano that matches the pitch of your speaking voice. You may be surprised at how low it is. Many women speak below middle C, even though they sing much higher.

What is the best pitch for speaking? Speech teachers recommend that you use a habitual pitch about one-third of the way up the scale from your lowest possible speaking tone to your highest. Observe your speaking pitch over a period of several days, noticing how high your voice goes when you are excited or surprised. The pitch of your voice when you laugh or cough also provides a clue to the most natural pitch for your speaking voice. When you find the best pitch level, it will help you speak without fatigue. Because your speaking pitch will vary with expression, it is not necessary to measure it exactly.

Does speaking too low or too high cause any problems? Yes, it can cause vocal fatigue and even voice loss. Also, our wish to speak low means that many persons start out singing in the heavy voice and feel uncomfortable about experimenting with the blended and light voices. Of course, the opposite can also be true, and some students need encouragement to use the strength that the heavy voice will give to their low notes.

Your voice teacher will encourage you to work on strengthening the weaker parts of your voice. A basic goal of voice training is to balance and strengthen all of the notes in your range.

## What kind of voice?

If you ask your teacher, "What kind of voice do I have?" you may receive an answer right away, or your teacher may prefer to wait and see how your voice develops over a period of time. A choral director classifies voices quickly in auditions, but voice teachers prefer to take more time.

Poor vocal habits and wrong ideas about singing can hide the natural quality of your voice so that it takes weeks or months for it to emerge. Some students imitate a favorite singer whose quality is not at all like their own. They are not deliberately faking; they simply think that their favorite singer's style is the best way to sing.

Imitation is a valid way of learning to sing, but only if the sound you imitate is right for you. Your voice is going to change and grow, but if you try to change it into something that is against its physical nature, there can be problems ahead. There are serious risks, for instance, if a woman, to help out her choir, sings tenor all the time. If you use one part of your range exclusively, you run a risk of overusing it and making the rest of your voice seem feeble by comparison. A good way to use your voice is to balance the use of the registers.

**Voice types**

To answer the question "What kind of voice do I have?" you need to know what names are given to different voices. In fact, voices have somewhat different names in different kinds of music.

Choral music uses four kinds of voices: *soprano, alto, tenor,* and *bass*. Any section can also divide into higher and lower voices, for instance, first altos and second altos (abbreviated Alto I and Alto II).

Opera requires more precise classifications of voices. Sopranos who specialize in singing notes above the staff are called coloratura or lyric-coloratura sopranos. Lower-voiced women are divided into *mezzo-sopranos*, who sing almost as high as sopranos, and *contraltos*, who specialize in low singing. Lower-voiced men are similarly divided into *baritones*, bass-baritones, and *basses*. In addition, operatic voices can be further classified by words that describe what the voice does best or how it sounds, such as lyric or dramatic. Opera fans love to discuss what kind of voice is best for a certain role on the basis of their interpretation of the character.

Broadway musical theater uses a different concept in classifying women's voices. Most roles require a woman to *belt*, which means to sing at a high energy level, especially in a low range. Some belting roles go even lower than an operatic contralto. On Broadway a blended or head tone is called "legitimate" or just "legit." A casting notice might read, "Must sing both belt and legit." The Broadway concept is that a woman chooses between belt and legit singing according to her natural ability, training, and personal preference. (Male voices can also belt, but the contrast between belt and legit is less striking in male voices because of the prevalence of chest tones.)

**Belt and pop singing**

Is belting dangerous? Many voice teachers think so. It is especially dangerous for young voices because their muscular development is not complete. Some voice teachers reject belting because they simply do not like the sound. Yet, if you accept a role in a musical, you may have to do some belting.

**Table 4.1**
Types of voices

| | Choral | Operatic/Concert | Pop/Broadway |
|---|---|---|---|
| **Women** | | | |
| (high) | | Coloratura soprano | |
| | Soprano | Soprano | Legit/soprano |
| | Alto | Mezzo-soprano | Belt |
| (low) | | Contralto | |
| **Men** | | | |
| (high) | Tenor | Tenor | Tenor |
| | | Baritone | |
| | Bass | Bass-baritone | Baritone |
| (low) | | Bass | |

Certainly, belting is a high-energy way of singing and carries some risks just like other high-energy activities, including singing opera or playing hockey. Some singers belt well and sing professionally on Broadway for years without losing their voices. Others belt poorly, ignore trouble signs such as hoarseness and pain, and lose their voices in a short time.

The same goes for both women and men who sing rock, jazz, or other kinds of popular music. Loud electronic instruments cause many young singers to force their voices and even lose them.

If you sing popular or Broadway music, please don't keep it a secret. Your teacher can help you to sing without hurting your voice.

## Finding your best resonance

**Resonance** means the intensification of a tone through sympathetic vibration, which is *the tendency of air in an enclosed or partially enclosed space to vibrate in response to a musical tone*. Here are examples: The tone of a vibrating guitar string is intensified by resonating inside the body of the guitar. The vibrating lips of a trumpeter produce a tone that is intensified by resonating inside the horn. Similarly, the tone made by your vocal cords resonates in your throat, mouth, and nose.

While making your voice louder, resonance strengthens the overtones that give your voice its basic quality. Overtones that produce vowel colors change with each change in the shape and size of your throat and mouth openings.

### *Increasing your resonance*

Stronger resonance means that your voice has more carrying power, more ability to seize and hold the attention of a listener, and more power to communicate your feelings.

Do you remember hearing a baby's cry? It instantly grabs your attention. Other powerful communicators are laughs, groans, whimpers, and sighs. These are all wordless emotional messages, and our brains instinctively give them attention. Singing takes some of the emotional power of these natural sounds, gives them musical form, and combines them with words. This understanding of the nature of singing gives us clues to discovering our best resonance.

Resonance arises instinctively when we

- really want to communicate,
- use emotional energy and enthusiasm,
- put physical energy into our sound, or
- get rid of physical and emotional blocks.

Experiment with the sentences that follow, speaking them out loud. Use enough energy to be heard in a large room. See how many different emotional meanings you can give to each one.

- Will you sing a solo?
- You should have been there!
- So you are the one!
- Hey you, get away from my car!

Can you make up other sentences that call up emotional responses? At this stage, let your feelings be the key to vocal resonance. In chapter 6 (on vowels), you will learn more about the technical side of resonance.

## Feeling and hearing

While your mental concepts about singing are developing, you can rely on the two senses that control singing, *feeling* and *hearing*, to know when you are on the right track. Ask yourself these questions as you sing:

- *Does your throat feel comfortable and relaxed?* If you feel tension, pressure, or pain in your throat, there is clearly something wrong.
- *Do you feel that the tone can be manipulated up or down in range, louder or softer in dynamics, darker or brighter in tone color?* A lack of flexibility in these three respects is a strong sign of unwanted tension.
- *Is the tone smooth, steady, and flowing, with an even vibrato?*
- *Is the tone ringing, intense ("hummy"), and efficient in resonance?*
- *Is the vowel clear and pure?*
- *Is the tone on pitch?*

*Relaxation and resonance*

Your best resonance usually goes along with a sense of freedom and relaxation. Tension in the tongue, jaw muscles, and neck, which are close to the larynx itself, will immediately impair ease, quality, and control of singing. Other body tensions may also interfere sooner or later. In a healthy throat, if the extrinsic (outer) muscles are relaxed, the intrinsic (inner) muscles of the larynx can do their job properly.

# Exercises

These exercises further help to eliminate physical tensions that can interfere with resonant singing. Although not everyone has the same tensions, all of these exercises help to warm up the voice. Combine them with exercises from chapters 1 and 2.

4.1 **Mental Messages.** Imagine the muscles under your eyes completely relaxed, the lips loose, the tongue lying forward in the mouth, and the jaw hanging freely. One by one, send mental messages to the cheeks, lips, tongue, and jaw to relax.

4.2 **Jaw Wobble.** Using both hands, move your jaw *gently* from side to side. The hands supply the movement, not the jaw muscles, which should be perfectly loose. If you cannot do this, work patiently with a mirror until you discover how to release the muscles that are holding the jaw stiff. (If this causes any discomfort, stop immediately and consult your dentist.)

4.3 **Jaw Flopper.** Shake your head easily from side to side, with the jaw and lips swinging loosely from side to side.

4.4 **Yes Nod.** Nod your head lazily up and down to relax your neck muscles. (Don't worry about looking silly; you are working to achieve needed relaxation.)

4.5 **Hand Shake.** Shake your hands loosely from the wrists, dispelling any tension in your arms.

Let your voice warm up on some of the vocal exercises from chapters 1 through 3 before going on to the next exercises. Some exercises cover a range of a full octave. Do you have a better understanding now of why high tones feel different from low tones?

**4.6.  Little Arches.** Even before you sing the first note, have the first *two* notes of each phrase in mind. If you do this, the upward jump will be in tune and the tones will connect smoothly. Purpose: to use breath and resonance evenly in a small melodic pattern. (High voices: Sing this in F Major, starting on b-flat.)

**4.7.  Octave Flip.** Start on any high, light note that comes easily to your voice. "Flip" to the low note and back up, that is, change pitches suddenly, allowing the clicking sound that one hears in yodelling. Transpose downward by half-steps a few times, then start over on a higher pitch. Purpose: to sense a contrast between the light and heavy registers in their pure forms, not mixed.

**4.8.  Octave Sigh.** Start on any high, light note that comes easily to your voice. Sing the word "sigh" and also feel that you really are sighing while your voice slides down one octave, passing through all of the notes without stopping on any. Begin the slide on the third beat of the measure. Transpose downward by half steps a few times, then start over on a higher pitch. Purpose: to smooth out and minimize the differences between the light and heavy registers, mixing them gradually on the way down.

**4.9.  5-Note Bee-dee's.** Start on any easy note around the midpoint of your range. Transpose downward to your lowest comfortable range. Purpose: to sense an easy, bright resonance, combined with quick, light articulation.

Bee - dee - bee - dee - bee - dee - bee - dee  -  bee - dee - bee - dee - bee.

**4.10.  5-Note Ee-Ah's.** Start on any easy note around the midpoint of your range. Sense the brightness of the first vowel and let the brightness carry into the second vowel. Transpose downward to your lowest comfortable range, then start over again a little higher. Purpose: to sense the way one vowel can brighten another.

*(Sing three times)*      *(Ending)*          *(Sing three times)*

Eee _____ Ah _____      Ah _____      Ee _____ Ah _____      Ah, _____

**4.11.  Focusers.** Try these combinations of syllables, which have been used by many singers to "center" their vocal energy. With your teacher's guidance, notice which ones work best for you and practice them daily. Transpose into several comfortable keys. Purpose: to experience the relationship between vowel and resonance, as well as the role of initial consonants in preparing tone.

Mm - oh,      mm - oh,      mm - oh,      mm - oh,      mm - oh.

*Additional reading*

*For tips on improving your speaking voice:*
*Is Your Voice Telling on You?* by Daniel R. Boone, Ph.D. Singular Publishing Group, San Diego, CA, 1991.

*For more of the technique and style of pop singing:*
*Born to Sing* by Elisabeth Howard and Howard Austin. Vocal Power Institute, 9826 Columbus Avenue, North Hills, CA 91343. (Available as a videocassette or as a book and cassette package.)

# 5 Preparing a Song

*Guiding questions:* *What is the best way to learn the words and music of songs so that I can sing them expressively and confidently?*

EVEN though there is much more to learn about vocal technique, you can begin to use what you know in songs. This book contains a large variety of songs that are fun to sing. They also give you an opportunity to learn more about your voice and about singing.

Your teacher may choose the first song you will learn or else help you choose it. Perhaps you will have a chance to hear several songs and select among them. If you are on your own, you could use the following advice about choosing a song.

1. *Choose words that you can believe in.* If words don't make sense to you, they are harder to learn, and it is harder to motivate yourself to sing expressively.

2. *Start out with easier songs* so that you can pay attention to improving your tone quality.

3. *Choose a short song* over a longer one. At first, you will learn more by doing several short songs than by sticking to one long one. Also, your teacher can give you more help in lessons if you sing a short song several times rather than a long song once.

After you have done several easy songs, the time will come to apply your skill to longer, more challenging songs. But now the main goal is to learn, quickly and pleasurably, how to sing.

In order to be sure you like the chosen song, you will want to *hear it* right away. Use your cassette recorder to tape the song in class. You can sing through some or all of the song, but only as long as it is easy and fun to do so. Let any hard parts wait until later.

Make a mental note of *something you really like* in your song because you are going to spend a lot of time with it. Does it appeal to you because of a mood, a mental picture, or an idea? Because of a graceful melody or a lively rhythm? Because of its quaintness or its modern sound?

You have made friends with your new song—why not start singing it? Simply because you don't want to make mistakes that will turn into habits. Also, singing in an insecure, uncertain way brings on tension that can turn into bad vocal habits. On the other hand, patient work now will pay off in confidence and success when we are ready to perform.

## Learning the tune

Let's work on a song together: "Love Will Find Out the Way," found on page 111. The way we learn this song will work for any song you want to sing.

First, take a good look at the music notation. The heading says that this is a traditional English song with a melody that was published as long ago as 1652.

Country folk have sung this tune for a long time, and this gives a clue to the mood and style of the song: vigorous, straightforward, uncomplicated. Of course, the tune originally was sung without any accompaniment; the piano part has been added especially for this book.

Rhythm provides a lot of the energy of this song. The underlying rhythm is in three-beat patterns: musicians say that the song is in triple meter, or three beats to the measure. Even without the *meter signature* of ¾, it would be clear that most measures have three syllables of text.

If you have learned to read notes and play an instrument, this song will be easy for you. If you do not play an instrument, you might record the song on a cassette in class or in your lesson. It works well to record the melody alone, then the piano part.

Notice that the piano part contains all of the notes of the melody. We say that the piano "doubles" the voice in this song, although not in all of the songs in this book. Doubling makes the song easy to learn but also limits the amount of freedom you have to interpret the song your own way.

While you listen to your tape of the melody, it is a good idea to "keep time" actively. This helps you develop a physical relationship to the music so that your rhythm will be steady and clear when you sing.

You could tap all the beats in the same spot, but you might forget which beat is which. Here is a better way to keep time: Sit at a table and tap the meter on the tabletop with one hand or both. Tap the three beats this way:

beat 1 near the book,

beat 2 a few inches away, and

beat 3 further away.

At the end of each measure return your hand to the starting position; the movement of your hand through the air gives extra energy to beat 1. If you use both hands, move them away from your body on beats 1, 2, and 3 and back to the starting position after beat 3.

Remember to tap the basic, steady beat. Don't try to beat the shorter and longer notes in the melody.

Now try tapping the meter steadily while listening to the melody. Most measures have notes on all three beats, but sometimes you are tapping a beat that does not have a note on it. For instance, the second syllable of "over" is lengthened so that "the" comes not on beat 3 but after it. "Waves" fills up a measure; be sure that the measure lasts its full length of three beats and is not accidentally shortened.

While you tap the meter steadily through the whole melody, you are learning it by ear. When you feel that the melody is familiar, try singing it on nonsense syllables. "Doo-doo-doo" and "La-la-la" are syllables that work well at this stage. (If you have learned to read notes and use the do-re-mi syllables, this is the time to make use of that knowledge.)

Singing the melody on syllables is called *vocalizing*, and it is a significant part of learning a song. Repeat this step just as many times as you need to feel perfectly confident about the melody. Your voice should feel easy and comfortable, and your breath support should be working well before you try to add the words to the song.

You may have noticed that the melody of "Love Will Find Out the Way" begins with a phrase that is repeated immediately and that the whole melody is only four phrases long. The melody will be sung over again for every stanza of the words. Most music has some such repetition patterns, and noticing these patterns is part of learning the music.

If at this point you want to know more about reading notes, you can always skip ahead on your own and read chapter 12, "A Vocabulary for Music."

# Learning
# the words

A wise person once said that *all* songs are love songs, and this song is about the power of love. We will begin with the poetry. Do you like poetry? If you're not sure, at least keep an open mind. Every song begins as a poem. Without words, how could we express what we want to sing about?

(Step 1) *Write out the poem by hand.* Why? When words are spread out under the notes of a melody, you can't see clearly how they fit together to form a poem and tell a story. As you write, most lines begin with capital letters and most lines end with rhyme words. Here is the first stanza of "Love Will Find Out the Way":

> Over the mountains
> And over the waves,
> Under the fountains
> And under the graves,
> Under floods that are deepest,
> Which Neptune obey,
> Over rocks that are steepest,
> Love will find out the way.

Finish writing out the other stanzas of the poem. By writing out the words we find that every line rhymes with one other line. This information makes it easier to memorize the poem.

(Step 2) *Make sure you understand every word* of the poem. One way to make sure is to *paraphrase* the poem, which means to express every idea of the poem in your own words. Either write out your paraphrase on paper or in your mind so that the meaning of every word and phrase you sing will be clear to you.

Paraphrases are in prose because the rhymes and rhythms don't matter, only the meanings. Change as many words as you can without changing the meaning. A paraphrase is usually longer than the poem because a good poem is concentrated into as few words as possible. And your paraphrase will be different from anyone else's because a poetic phrase can have more than one meaning. Besides, a good poem always communicates on more than one level, including the musical effects of rhythm and rhyme.

Are there unfamiliar words? Let your dictionary help you. (Do you need to look up Neptune?) No one knows every word in the English language, and even a current Broadway lyric might have expressions that you haven't heard before.

Here is a sample paraphrase of the stanza printed above:

> Wherever a lover needs to go: over earth or sea; or under the earth; or under the waves of the sea, which are obedient to the sea god; or over steep, rocky hills—a lover will succeed in getting to the beloved.

(Step 3) *Decide what is the main point* of the poem, the chief message that you will convey to your listeners. At this point you personalize the poem and decide what role you are playing when you sing it. Are you singing your own words or someone else's? When you sing "Love Will Find Out the Way," are you a philosopher expressing an opinion? Or are you waiting hopefully for someone to find you and fall in love with you? Or are you a lover yourself, and you want everyone to know that you will stop at nothing to win your love?

(Step 4) *Read the poem aloud with expression, phrasing, and accentuation.* Find the words that communicate action and feeling because those words will give the song *expression*. "Smiles," "revives," and "delight" are energy words.

Find the *phrasing* because your breathing will depend on it when you sing. For instance, you will probably connect the first two lines of the poem together and sing them in one breath.

Notice the correct *accentuation* of the poem because it may give you clues about the musical rhythm.

Now (Step 5) *speak the poem aloud rhythmically.* Tap the beat, three beats to a measure, just as you did while learning the melody. Let each word have its full time; for instance, in "Over the mountains . . ." the second word needs a full beat. Ignore the fact that the beat is broken into two eighth-notes.

When you practice rhythmic speaking, several things happen at once: you are practicing the rhythm, memorizing the words, learning to articulate the words in time, and training your eye to move along the line of words so that it is always just ahead of the word you are saying.

Rhythmic speaking needs to be done with your voice at a little higher pitch than usual because your singing voice is probably even higher. Let your voice sound alive and loving, not low energy.

Work through all of the stanzas of the song, taking time to do this stage correctly. Go slowly enough to keep the rhythms clear, accurate, and easy. You are forming vocal habits and breathing habits that will make the song easier when you are ready to sing it. The only missing element of the song is the melody.

## Phrasing

How will you get any breath to sing? You may always breathe at a rest sign. For a singer, a rest sign does not mean "rest," it means "breathe."

But this song has no rest signs. How do you decide when to breathe? Let the words guide you. The words have to make sense. If you pay attention to the meaning of the words, you will never breathe in the middle of a word or breathe between words that have to connect with each other to make sense. Punctuation will often guide you.

When you know where you want to breathe, just shorten the preceding note and take your breath so that you can begin the next phrase on time. For instance, at the end of the first phrase the word "waves" must be sung for only two beats instead of three. On the third beat you will breathe and then start the next phrase on time.

If you have a question about phrasing, go back to reading the poem aloud in a natural way. Wherever you can breathe while speaking the poem, you can breathe when you sing it.

Sometimes breathing points are indicated in songs with written signs above the staff, either a wedge (v) or a comma (,) or with long curved lines called phrase marks. If a song needs different phrasing marks for the second stanza, they might be printed with the words instead of being over the music.

### Catch breaths

Sometimes the meaning requires a quick breath, called a *catch breath.* For instance, if you take a catch breath after "steepest," there will be a stronger emphasis on the next word, "Love." (The syllable "-est" is shortened to make time for the breath.)

Do you still practice "Starter" (exercise 2.7)? You learned to take small amounts of breath using the correct physical action, and now is the time to use that skill.

When you have all the rhythms and breathing points worked out, play your audiocassette of the accompaniment while you speak the poem in rhythm. You're almost ready to sing, but do this step first. When you can speak your poem exactly in rhythm with the recorded accompaniment, you can be satisfied that you really understand the rhythm of your song.

## Singing the song

When you have mastered the rhythms, the melody, and the words, you are ready to sing the song. All that is left is (Step 7): *combine the melody with the words.* You were already singing the melody with nonsense syllables; now you use words instead and adjust the phrasing so that the words continue to make sense.

You can probably sing this song confidently by now, or you soon will be able to. With more difficult songs you might need to repeat some of the steps already done and work things out by yourself. Then you are ready to memorize the song and give all of your attention to expression. Chapter 9, "Performing a Song," will tell you more about sharing your song with an audience.

## Exercises

Although this chapter was not about vocal technique, it suggests some exercises to improve the musical quality of our singing. We will work on ear training, phrasing, and dynamics.

5.1  **Do-Re-Mi Scale.** We all know these syllables from Rodgers and Hammerstein's song "Do-Re-Mi" in *The Sound of Music.* Sing either the English pronunciation:

do, re, mi, fa, so, la, ti, do

or the slightly different Italian version:

dɔ, rɛ, mi, fa, sɔ, la, si, dɔ

as your teacher prefers. Purpose: to sing long tones with close attention to intonation.

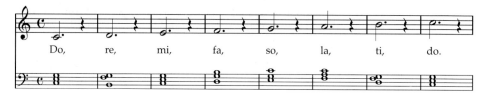

5.2  **2-Note Sighs.** Connect these pairs of tones smoothly. Purpose: to practice the syllables with clear intonation and easy catch breaths.

Do you sense that the pitches do and ti are closer to each other than the pitches ti-la, la-so, and so-fa? Also that fa and mi are closer to each other than mi-re and re-do? This may not be immediately clear, but with practice you will realize that do-ti and fa-mi are half steps and that the others are whole steps. Recognizing the half steps helps us to sing accurately in tune.

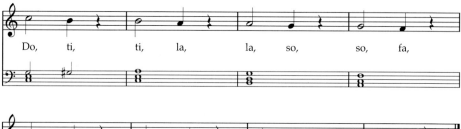

**5.3** **3-Note Sighs.** Connect these groups of tones smoothly. Purpose: the same as in exercise 5.2.

**5.4** **Swell.** In order to sing expressively you have to be able to sing louder and softer. Begin with just three clear levels, soft (p), medium (mf), and loud (f). Avoid "super-soft" and "super-loud" for now. Use consonants to help you make the gradations. Purpose: to realize that different volume levels are available throughout the voice.

*Additional reading*     *If you like poetry and want to know more about it, you would enjoy this attractive collection:*
*The Classic Hundred: All-Time Favorite Poems,* edited by William Harmon. Columbia University Press, 1990.

# 6 Vowels and Vocal Color

*Guiding questions:* *How can I sing so that everyone understands my words? Can I sing the way I speak or do I have to change words to sing them? How can I color my voice so that there is variety in my singing?*

DO you like to hear people speak a language you do not understand? Or are you bored? It may be fun to hear a few sentences in an unfamiliar language, but we usually grow bored with sounds that we can't understand.

When we hear a singer whose words are unclear, the experience is much the same. We try to catch what information we can, but soon our minds wander. We miss a large part of the pleasure that we should get from the song.

Why does this happen?

First, some singers simply don't realize that others are not understanding their words.

Also, many people have not learned to pronounce the English language distinctly and beautifully.

Most of us have some regional speech habits that are distracting or unclear to people from other areas. We may find to our surprise that we use pronunciations that others consider wrong. We need to learn Standard American pronunciation, which sounds correct and appropriate to any English-speaking person in the United States or Canada.

## Your speaking voice

*Singing is, first of all, saying.* This maxim contains one of the keys to moving the emotions of an audience. Your listeners can be persuaded only if they understand what you say.

*If your speaking voice is free and resonant, it furnishes the best foundation and model for singing.* The other side of the coin is that if your speaking voice is not free and resonant—if it is timid, breathy, or dull or if you have an unpleasant regional twang or drawl—then your singing will suffer, too. Be open to the possibility that your speaking voice needs work in order to release the full potential of your singing voice.

To sing clearly is definitely more difficult than to speak clearly. Music inevitably alters language sounds by

- stretching short vowels over long notes;
- giving full length and tone to syllables that might be very weak, or even omitted, in conversational speech; and
- carrying the voice higher than it goes in normal speech. (Certain vowels become indistinguishable from each other on higher notes of the female voice.)

These problems can be overcome with knowledge, awareness, and thoughtful practice.

## What is diction?

**Diction** is the area of vocal technique related to making words clear. It includes several concepts that are summed up in this sentence: *"We pronounce words, enunciate vowels and syllables, and articulate consonants."* When we do all of these well, we have good diction.

As a performer, you may use various styles of diction, informal and formal. If you are going to perform in blue jeans, then your hometown accent will sound fine. If the performance requires dressing up or wearing a costume, then your diction should be "dressed up" also. Let your diction match the style of the occasion and the needs of the performance.

Will you have to change your speaking voice? Changing something so personal may worry you. Will people think you sound phony?

Actually, you don't need to change your everyday speaking voice unless you want to or unless your speech habits are unhealthful. You don't have to give up your familiar way of speaking when you learn new techniques for singing.

## The International Phonetic Alphabet (IPA)

In school we learned five vowel letters: *a, e, i, o, u,* and sometimes *y.*

As singers, we need to think in terms of *sounds* rather than letters. In this book from now on the word *vowel* means vowel sound. English has far more than five vowel sounds. For the extra vowels we will borrow symbols from the International Phonetic Alphabet, abbreviated IPA.

*Phonetics* is the scientific study of speech sounds. Scholars of phonetics need symbols with which they can take written notes about the sounds of any language. The IPA serves that purpose, in that each IPA symbol stands for only one sound and never for any other. When you have learned IPA symbols in English, they will be very useful in studying other languages as well.

The IPA lets us analyze words and write down, or *transcribe*, the sounds of a word or a whole text.

IPA transcriptions contain symbols only for the sounds that can be heard, but no symbols for silent letters and punctuation. Do not use capital letters because sometimes small and capital letters have different meanings in the IPA.

When IPA symbols occur in a normal context, they are enclosed in square brackets. The brackets can enclose a letter, a word, or a whole text. Here is an example:

The sound [ju] is spelled one way in cute [kjut] and another way in pew [pju].

Actors, announcers, and speech teachers all rely on Kenyon and Knott's *A Pronouncing Dictionary of American English,* which gives all pronunciations in IPA. Pronunciations given in this book all follow Kenyon and Knott's standard. If you are used to some other pronunciations, just be aware that they are not Standard American and might cause confusion.

All of the IPA symbols used in this book are listed for reference in Appendix B, page 272.

## Vowels for singing

Vowels are vocal sounds that are made with a *free, unrestricted flow of breath.* They differ from consonants, which all obstruct the air in one way or another.

To make the various vowels, the lips and tongue change the shape of the mouth and throat resonators without stopping the breath flow. (The vocal cords may also influence vowels, but voice scientists are not sure about this because of the difficulty of precisely measuring the vocal cords while they are in motion.)

Every vowel can be described as a *bright, neutral, or dark vowel.* These qualities are inherent in the vowels when they are correctly produced. For instance, a well-produced bright vowel is naturally that way; you don't have to exert yourself to make it bright.

In each category, vowels can also be described as being *closed or open*, referring to how low the jaw is dropped and to the way the tongue is lifted or not lifted toward the roof of the mouth (palate). No vowel is completely closed, and most vowels are more open for singing than for speech.

All vowels *can resonate freely*, and singers train themselves to have a uniform sensation of vibration for all vowels. This sensation is at odds with speech theory, which often refers to "front vowels," "midvowels," and "back vowels." Such terms refer to the part of the tongue that is active in shaping the mouth resonator; it has nothing to do with the vibratory sensations experienced by good singers. This book does not use the term "back vowel" because it might mislead a student into making a throaty tone.

All vowels can be produced with the *tip of the tongue lightly touching the lower teeth*. Most singers find this position helpful for vocal relaxation.

Finally, all vowels *can be prolonged* for as long as the music requires. In school we learned long and short vowels, but in singing all vowels are as long as we want them to be.

## The seven Italian vowels

Because Italians were the first to invent opera and to export singing stars to other nations, classical vocal study has traditionally emphasized the Italian language. Some teachers recommend that their students sing their first songs in Italian because Italian has only a few different vowels. For these reasons we highlight the seven vowels that are used in Italian. (The way the vowels are numbered below matches the numbers in the list of IPA symbols on page 272.)

The seven Italian vowels are as follows:

| IPA symbol: | English name: | Some possible spellings: |
|---|---|---|
| 1. [i] | Ee | bee, sea, brief, machine |
| 3. [e] | Pure Ay | chaotic, dictates |
| 4. [ɛ] | Open Eh | met, less, head, said |
| 6. [a] | Bright Ah | aisle (British: ask, dance) |
| 9. [ɔ] | Open O (or Aw) | ought, dawn, haul, wall |
| 10. [o] | Pure Oh | hotel, obey |
| 12. [u] | Oo | true, who, moo, few, through |

## Tongue vowels

The four tongue vowels are differentiated from one another by the height of the tongue. The lips may either smile or stay relaxed.

1. [i], *Ee*, is the brightest of all vowels and the one with the least space between the tongue and palate. While the tip of the tongue touches the lower teeth, the tongue rises forward until it is close to the upper teeth. We say "smile and say cheese," but in fact you can "say cheese" perfectly well without smiling at all.

In singing [i], the mouth space usually needs to be larger than in speaking, but the opening is still smaller than for any other vowel. For acoustical reasons, a pure [i] is not resonant on high pitches. Most sopranos substitute [e] on high notes for the sake of greater comfort and stronger resonance with no loss of clarity.

3. [e], *Pure Ay*, is also a bright vowel, and its degree of openness is about halfway between [i] and [a]. More about this vowel later.

4. [ɛ], *Open Eh*, is bright but more open than [e]. The tongue rises forward, but only a little.

6. [a], *Bright Ah*, is the most open of the Italian vowels. It is the true "Italian ah." In order to discover it, say all of the bright vowels in order, opening them gradually: [i, e, ɛ, a], so that the tongue is very slightly forward of its resting position.

Standard American pronunciation does not use Bright Ah by itself, although it is used by some British as well as some easterners and southerners. In chapter 8 we will see how important Bright Ah is in diphthongs.

Whenever [a] occurs in British pronunciation, standard American uses [æ], as in "chaff," "laugh," "command," "branch," "nasty," and "mast." If you ever want to sound British, as in singing *Pirates of Penzance* or *Camelot,* sing [a] instead of [æ] in such words.

*Lip vowels*

12. [u], *Oo,* is the darkest of all vowels. A safe, easy way to darken [u] is to round the lips. Let your tongue relax and touch the lower teeth. Most singers find it easy to sing [u] softly because of its natural darkness, but for projection of a strong tone it may be necessary to open [u] somewhat toward [o].

Many Americans speak [u] without rounding the lips; they get the necessary closure by tensing and lifting the back of the tongue instead. Your [u] will be more beautiful and comfortable if you sing it with rounded lips and relaxed tongue. Think of [u] as a "hollow" sound, with a lot of space in the mouth.

10. [o], *Pure Oh,* is a dark vowel, and its degree of openness is about halfway between [a] and [u]. More about this vowel later.

9. [ɔ], *Open O,* is also dark but much more open than [o]. An easy way to darken [ɔ] is to round your lips slightly. This vowel is a favorite of many singers for vocalizing.

Unfortunately, many Americans grow up in areas where [ɔ] is never heard in daily speech. Say these pairs of words out loud: "hock" and "hawk"; "la" and "law"; "sod" and "sawed"; "cot" and "caught." The second word in each pair contains [ɔ]. If the paired words sound identical to your ears, you are among those whose speech lacks the [ɔ] sound. Practice saying "hawk," "law," "sawed," and "caught" with your lips rounded in order to get used to this new sound. Again, you don't have to change your daily speech unless you want to, but welcome this new vowel into your vocabulary for the sake of good singing.

*Pure Ay and Pure Oh in English*

From a singer's point of view, Ay and Oh are seldom pure vowels in English. If you say Ay very slowly and listen carefully, you will hear the vowel sound change as you end it. And if you say Oh carefully, it will also change the end. (You will also feel movement in your mouth as the vowels change.) Such combinations of two vowels, called *diphthongs,* are discussed in chapter 8.

Do we always make diphthongs out of Ay and Oh? Nearly always, especially when we speak slowly or when the vowels are in strong, stressed syllables. But Ay and Oh remain pure when we speak rapidly or when they are in weak (unstressed) syllables, as in the example words above. Our ears interpret Pure Ay and Pure Oh as exact equivalents to their diphthong forms.

If the pure vowel and the diphthong are so much alike, why do we need to distinguish between them? Because English requires the diphthong and sounds artificial without it, and yet other languages require the pure vowel.

Music slows words down so much that every detail can be heard, and every language has its own distinctive sounds.

To sing in Italian you need all seven vowels described so far: [i, e, ɛ, a, ɔ, o, u]. To sing church Latin you need these five: [i, ɛ, a, ɔ, u]. To sing Spanish you need these five: [i, e, a, o, u].

*Eight English vowels*

The remaining vowels are so characteristic of English that they are difficult for most foreigners. Because we learned most of them as "short" vowels in spoken English, we have to focus carefully on their exact quality when they are stretched long by music. We will vocalize on the ones we need and become comfortable with them.

| IPA symbol: | English name: | Some possible spellings: |
| --- | --- | --- |
| 2. [ɪ] | Short I | sing, rely, been, women, busy |
| 5. [æ] | Short A | sang, mash, marry, cat, carry |
| 7. [ɑ] | Dark Ah | father, far, wander, watch |
| 8. [ɒ] | Short O | cot, sorry, hock, gone |
| 11. [ʊ] | Short U | full, put, good, would, woman |
| 13. [ʌ] | Uh | "... but young love does flood ..." |
| 14. [ə] | Schwa | *a* cactus, th*e* nation, |
| 15. [ɜ] | Er | serve, earth, girl, worth, hurt |

2. [ɪ], *Short I,* is a bright vowel, a little more open than [i], but similar to it when well sung.

Many Americans speak [ɪ] with the tongue pulled back, especially before or after [l], as in "little" or "ill." When this happens, the beauty and special color of the [ɪ] are lost. Practice saying [ɪ] with the tongue touching the lower teeth, and then say "sill" with the same clear vowel quality.

5. [æ], *Short A,* is a bright, open vowel. Some people shy away from the brightness of [æ], but it can be beautiful if the mouth opens freely and the tongue lies forward and relaxed.

[æ] has a bad reputation because it is usually spoken with unnecessary tension and/or nasality. Singers and choir directors often try so hard to avoid this ugliness that they change [æ] to [ɑ], so that "a man's hand" becomes "a mahn's hahnd." This is not a British accent; it is just unclear and affected. Remember that Shakespeare wrote *Hamlet,* not *Hahmlet.*

7. [ɑ], *Dark Ah,* lies in the center of the vowel color range. It is the most open of all vowels, meaning that the tongue lies quite low in the mouth, with the jaw comfortably open.

Because it is so open, [ɑ] is the vowel of choice for female singers' high notes. It can take on various shades of color, depending on the mood of the song. Individual speakers may use a variety of colors for this vowel, depending on their regional origin and preference. In order to find the normal or "real" [ɑ], which is exactly in the center of the color range, alternate [ɑ] with brighter and darker vowels: exercise 6.3 does this.

8. [ɒ], *Short O,* is a vowel that is recognized by some speech texts, but when it is lengthened by music, it sounds just like [ɑ]. Instead of vocalizing on [ɒ], we will sing [ɑ] instead.

11. [ʊ], *Short U,* is the second darkest vowel, after [u], and it is only slightly more open than [u]. Practice it as you do [u], with your tongue touching the lower teeth and a feeling of hollowness in your mouth. Unlike [ɒ], this vowel keeps its quality even in singing.

13. [ʌ], *Uh,* or "Ugh" if you prefer, is a moderately open neutral vowel. If someone hits you suddenly in the abdomen, this might be the sound that comes out. It is the fundamental sound of the human voice when the mouth and pharynx are not intentionally adjusted. It is so easy to sing that some singers habitually sing [ʌ] when they mean to sing [ɑ]. Many vocal exercises in this book use this vowel because it is so open and relaxed. Again, let the tongue relax forward to touch the lower teeth.

14. [ə], *Schwa,* is always short and always weak (unstressed). It is a neutral vowel, a little less open than [ʌ]. [ə] changes according to its neighbors: it is brighter in a happy mood or with bright vowels around it; it is darker in a somber mood or with dark vowels around it. It is more open if it occurs between open vowels, more closed between closed vowels.

When we lengthen [ə] for singing, it usually sounds most like vowel 13 [ʌ]. If we were asked to vocalize a phrase on a schwa, we would use [ʌ].

Despite its weakness, [ə] deserves special study because contrast between strong and weak syllables is characteristic of English. In some languages (French and Japanese, for instance) all syllables have equal strength, but not in English. A singer who ignores this fact and sings all syllables with equal strength sounds laborious and monotonous.

Schwas occur often. Slowly say this sentence aloud; every word contains a schwa: "The handsome captain salutes a respected woman." As you can see, various vowel letters can be used to spell a schwa.

The name "schwa" comes from a Hebrew alphabet sign, *shva*, which usually indicates a weak vowel just like ours. Sometimes it shows that there is no vowel where one might be expected. English also has words in which we see a vowel letter but leave it out in pronunciation as well as words in which no vowel is written but one must be sung. Here are some examples transcribed into IPA to show how they must be sung.

|         | Said:    | Should be sung: |
|---------|----------|-----------------|
| cotton  | [kɑtn]   | [kɑtən]         |
| bottom  | [bɑtm]   | [bɑtəm]         |
| little  | [lɪtl]   | [lɪtəl]         |
| didn't  | [dɪdnt]  | [dɪdənt]        |

In chapter 8 you will learn more about [ə] and its role in a family of schwa-diphthongs.

15. [ɜ], *Er*, is also a neutral vowel, like vowels 13 and 14, but it is less open and somewhat darkened. When most people hear this sound, they are less aware of the vowel than of the *r* that is present in its spelling.

[ɜ], like vowel 5 [æ], has a bad reputation because so many people sing it with tension and an ugly tone. An angry dog says "Grr," and some people go almost that far with this vowel.

To find a beautiful form of [ɜ], sing it like the other dark vowels. Let your lips round slightly. Let your tongue lie low and forward in your mouth while the middle of the tongue rises a little. Above all, avoid bunching up the back of your tongue as many people do when saying [r].

We can vocalize on [ɜ] if we completely remove all trace of [r] quality from the vowel. Practice saying "earth" and "hers" with no [r] at all. When sung well, this vowel is practically identical with the French vowel in *jeune* and the German vowel in *könnte*. Once found, [ɜ] is an easy vowel for most voices to vocalize.

# Equalizing the vowels

Almost everyone finds some vowels easier and stronger than others; our goal in exercising is to sing all vowels with equal comfort and strong resonance while we also give each vowel its own special sound. Because it is the most basic sound of the voice, we often use vowel 13 [ʊ] for a comparison with other vowels and adjust their resonance to be like it.

For the sake of evenness in singing, let your mouth open moderately for all vowels. Open vowels are likely to be naturally louder than closed vowels. Avoid over-opening the naturally open vowels [æ, ɑ]. Open up the closed vowels [i, ɪ, u, ʊ] much more than would seem right for their pure quality. Let [ʌ] be your model.

Also, for the sake of evenness, avoid exaggerated mouth positions, such as grinning. Once you understand what the various vowels are, form them as easily as possible.

## Coloring your voice for expression

In infancy we learned that bright vocal colors go with a smiling face and that dark vocal colors go with a scowling face. Unconsciously, adult listeners also sense a relationship between facial expressions and vocal sounds.

Bright vowels sung with a smiling face enhance the sound of a happy song. For a more somber mood, the bright vowels can be sung with the lips relaxed. If your higher tones have a bright, edgy quality or if you want to add a soothing quality to words such as "peace" or "sleep," you can reduce the brightness of [i] by rounding your lips in the direction of [u].

Dark vowels sung with rounded lips bring out the mood of a serious song. For a happier mood, or if listeners tell you that your vocal quality is too dark, you can practice saying and singing these vowels with a smile. Try the word "jovial."

*Summary of fifteen vowels*

Vowels 1–6 [i, ɪ, e, ɛ, æ, a] are all bright vowels, which require the tongue to lift and move forward. Use either smiling or relaxed lips.

Vowels 8–12 [ɒ, ɔ, o, ʊ, u] are all dark vowels; let the tongue remain low and relaxed. Let the lips round and darken the vowels, without tongue tension.

Vowels 7 and 13–15 [ɑ, ʌ, ə, ɜ] are all neutral vowels that allow great variety of coloration according to mood. They can be made darker with lip-rounding or brighter with smiling, while still remaining understandable.

# Exercises

Among the fifteen English vowel sounds there are three that we do not vocalize, because in singing

- [a] always changes into either [æ] or [ɑ];
- [ɒ] changes to [ɑ] when sustained; and
- [ə] changes to [ʌ] when sustained.

We will put off vocalizing vowel 3 [e] and vowel 10 [o] until we study them as diphthongs in chapter 8.

These exercises use the ten remaining vowel sounds. Our basic exercise method is to sound vowels next to each other in groups of two or three. Compare and contrast them for yourself, and check your observations with your teacher and your fellow students.

From this point on, our vocal exercises will use IPA symbols, except when whole English words are used. The consonants used here are pronounced with normal English sounds.

6.1   **Bright Vowels.** Sing smoothly, with clear vowel qualities and even dynamics. These vowels are in the words "me," "muss," "miss," "mess," and "mat." Purpose: to establish the bright vowels and to compare each one with [ʌ].

6.2 **Dark Vowels.** Sing smoothly, just as in the last exercise. These vowels are in the words "do," "good," and "law." Purpose: to establish the dark vowels and to compare each one with [ʌ].

6.3 **Row with Ah.** Tongue tend to brighten your vocal sound and lip vowels tend to darken it. Purpose: to equalize [a] so that it is neither too bright nor too dark.

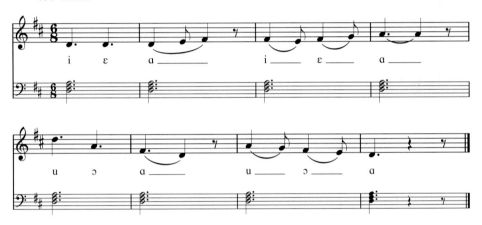

6.4 **Nonsense waltz.** Sing smoothly. For fun, put emotions into these nonsense words, singing as if you were angry, jealous, giddy, and so on. Purpose: to establish *legato* singing in vowels that English and Italian have in common.

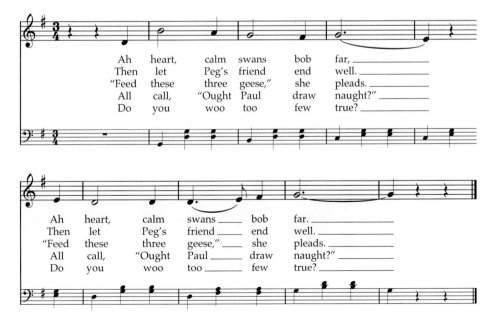

**6.5   Tri-puh-lets.** Avoid any sound of consonant *r* in the second syllable. Purpose: to establish [ɜ] as a singable vowel with no consonant character.

ma ——— mɜ ——— ma          ma ——— mɜ ——— ma
si ——— sɜ ——— si          si ——— sɜ ——— si
bu ——— bɜ ——— bu          bu ——— bɜ ——— bu

**6.6   Vowel Cousins.** The following pairs of vowels have the same degree of opening. They help to "tune" each other; in other words, improvement in one vowel also leads to improvement in the other one.

i __ u __ i          u __ i __ u          i __ u __ i          u __ i __ u
ɪ __ ʊ __ ɪ          ʊ __ ɪ __ ʊ          ɪ __ ʊ __ ɪ          ʊ __ ɪ __ ʊ
ɛ __ ɔ __ ɛ          ɔ __ ɛ __ ɔ          ɛ __ ɔ __ ɛ          ɔ __ ɛ __ ɔ
æ __ ʌ __ æ          ʌ __ æ __ ʌ          æ __ ʌ __ æ          ʌ __ æ __ ʌ

*Additional reading*

*For clear, humorous, and thorough instruction about singing words clearly:*
*The Singer's Manual of English Diction* by Madeleine Marshall. Schirmer Books, New York, 1953.

*Singers, actors and broadcasters rely on:*
*A Pronouncing Dictionary of American English* by John S. Kenyon and Thomas A. Knott. G. & C. Merriam Co., Springfield, MA, 1953.

# 7 Consonants and Clarity

*Guiding questions:*

*How important are consonants? When I sing, will consonants help or get in the way? What if several consonants come together? Will they make my singing sound choppy?*

COMMON courtesy tells us to speak so that others can understand us. We have learned not to mumble or shout; we speak as clearly as we need to without overdoing. We will try to sing just that clearly, with the difference that we may want to sing in a large room for many people.

Some singers try so hard to energize their vocal tone that they forget to energize their consonants. If your singing tone suddenly becomes strong enough to hear 100 feet away, then the consonants need to be reinforced to carry across the same distance. Some consonants carry almost as strongly as vowel tones, but others are weak and must be exaggerated in order to be heard.

Aside from clear diction, some consonants actually help us to improve tone and clarify vowel quality. That's why we have already done a number of exercises that included consonant sounds.

Most IPA symbols for consonants are the same as normal alphabet letters. When you have learned the few new ones that are needed, you will be able to write whole words in IPA.

## Glides

Standard American has two sounds that resemble vowels in that they are "made with an unrestricted flow of breath," but they function as consonants because they always precede other vowels. They are called semiconsonants, or semivowels, and they are also called *glides* because of the smooth motion of the articulators in saying them.

(The way the consonants are numbered below matches the numbers in the list of IPA symbols on page 272.)

| IPA symbol: | English name: | Some possible spellings: |
| --- | --- | --- |
| 16. [ j ] | Yah | you, yes, unit, few, Europe |
| 17. [w] | Wah | water, weed, wail, whoa!, one |

16. [ j ], *Yah*, begins from an [i] position, with the tongue lifted forward. Say "you" in slow motion, slowly enough to hear the sound of [i] as you begin and the change that occurs as your tongue moves from [i] to [u], the main vowel of "you."

Notice that *u* and *ew* sometimes have the sound of [ju], even though no letter is present to represent the [ j ]. There also is a large group of words in which [ j ] is optional for everyday speech, but required for "dress-up" speech. (Do you remember the distinction we made between "blue jeans" singing and "formal" singing?) The following pronunciations may sound peculiar to you, but they are appropriate for formal singing.

| Spelling: | IPA: | Examples: |
|-----------|------|-----------|
| *du, dew* | [dju] | due, dew, endure, duke |
| *lu* | [lju] | lute, allure (but not if a consonant precedes "l," as in "flute" or "blue") |
| *nu, new* | [nju] | new, news, nude, inure |
| *su, sew* | [sju] | suit, sewer, sue (but not "Susan") |
| | [zju] | resume |
| *tu* | [tju] | tune, Tuesday, student, stupid |
| *th* | [θju] | enthusiasm |

17. [w], *Wah*, begins from a [u] position, with rounded lips. Say "we" in slow motion, slowly enough to hear the sound of [u] as you begin and the change that occurs as your tongue moves from [u] to [i], the main vowel.

When you sing a word that starts with a voiced glide, be sure that it starts on pitch. If a glide starts below the pitch and slides up, it sounds lazy and careless.

## Consonants

What all consonants have in common is that they all interfere with our breath flow in some way and to some degree. The interference can occur at one of these locations:

- at the lips,
- between the lower lip and the upper teeth,
- between the tongue and the teeth,
- between the tongue and the ridge behind the teeth (called the gum ridge), or
- between the tongue and the hard palate.

The lips, teeth, tongue, and palate are called articulators because of their role in articulating consonants.

The most important thing to notice about any consonant sound is whether it is *voiced or unvoiced,* or whether the vocal bands vibrate during the sound. If they are vibrating, then the consonant has a musical pitch. If they are not vibrating, then the consonant is a noise that has no definite musical pitch.

How can you check whether a consonant is voiced? Either feel your larynx while you say the consonant, or stop one ear with a finger so that you hear the vibrations that come up through your throat from the vocal bands.

An easy one to test is [s], which is merely a noise and sounds the same with your ear stopped or open. Contrast it with [z]; the buzzing sensation that comes from your vocal bands is very noticeable when you feel your larynx or stop an ear.

Check every consonant as you read about it, and decide whether it is voiced or unvoiced. Voiced consonants, just like vowels and glides, must be kept on pitch and not allowed to slide up from below.

## Hums

We have three "hums," all of them voiced. They are different from other consonants because breath moves only through the nose rather than the mouth.

| IPA symbol: | English name: | Some possible spellings: |
|-------------|---------------|--------------------------|
| 18. [m] | Em | ma, summer, rim |
| 19. [n] | En | now, inner, ban |
| 20. [ŋ] | Ing | singer, finger, angry, anchor |

Test each hum to find out where it interferes with the breath. At the lips? At the gum ridge? Farther back on the palate?

Hums are useful to warm up the voice quietly. Hum with an even but economical flow of breath. If your hum sounds breathy, the vocal bands are not working efficiently. Stopping one ear with a finger, you can easily check your tone both for evenness and for clarity. Hums are so much like vowels that some teachers recommend to make them last at least twice as long in singing as they do in speech.

At the end of a word, many westerners confuse Ing with En. Words like "singing" should rhyme with "king" and not with "queen." All hums should end with a "clean release" and no extra vowel sound.

## Pairs of consonants

Most English consonants have partners; that is, an unvoiced consonant and a voiced one are produced by the same articulators in the same way. For instance, in the list below, [f] and [v] are produced in exactly the same way except that [f] is unvoiced and [v] is voiced.

Numbers 25–32 are *continuant* consonants, which can be prolonged easily. Numbers 33–40 are all *stop* consonants; they momentarily stop the flow of air.

| IPA symbol: | English name: | Some possible spellings: |
| --- | --- | --- |
| 25. [f] | Eff | fa, often, phrase, laugh |
| 26. [v] | Vee | vigor, over, verve |
| 27. [θ] | Theta | thin, Cathy, path |
| 28. [ð] | Edh | this, either, without, smooth |
| 29. [s] | Ess | solo, essence, kiss, science |
| 30. [z] | Zee | zoo, hazard, present, has |
| 31. [ʃ] | Shah | show, social, nation, sure |
| 32. [ʒ] | Zsa-Zsa | azure, pleasure, massage |
| 33. [p] | Pee | peach, upper, cup |
| 34. [b] | Bee | beach, baby, cub |
| 35. [t] | Tee | teach, atom, cut |
| 36. [d] | Dee | do, odor, head |
| 37. [k] | Kay | keep, tack, calm, accurate |
| 38. [g] | Hard Gee | go, again, tag |
| 39. [tʃ] | Cha-Cha | church, achieve |
| 40. [dʒ] | Soft Gee | gem, jelly, ridge, rajah |

Consonants vary in carrying power from [s], which can be clearly heard even in the softest whisper, to [p], the weakest of all consonants. For public speaking or singing, unvoiced consonants often need an extra burst of air, called an *aspiration*. This is what conductors mean when they say "Spit out your consonants!" Unfortunately, that command often causes choral singers to use more facial tension instead of using more breath.

A special word about the six stops, 33–38: a stop at the end of a word may not be heard unless we add an extra sound. For instance, if you end a word like "sleep" with your lips closed, the word hardly sounds different from "sleet" or "sleek."

For an unvoiced final [p], [t], or [k], add aspiration. Practice "sap, sat, sack" with a small burst of air after each final consonant. You can mark final stops this way: "sip[h]."

The voiced finals [b], [d], and [g] all need a weak schwa for carrying power on the release. Practice singing "rib, rid, rig" with a weak vowel after each final consonant—on pitch, of course! (The hum consonants do not need this extra sound if they are well resonated.)

Just like vowels, voiced consonants must begin and end on pitch, without a glottal attack or any extra sound afterward, except for the special case of final [b], [d], and [g].

# Special consonants

There are some remaining consonants that do not fit the pattern of voiced-unvoiced partners.

| IPA symbol: | English name: | Some possible spellings: |
| --- | --- | --- |
| 21. [l] | El | la, follow, sill |
| 22. [r] | Ahr | rib, arrow, far |
| 23. [h] | Aitch | hum, aha! |
| 24. [hw] | Which | what whale? |

21. [l], *El*, is made when the pointed tip of the tongue lightly and quickly touches the upper teeth or the gum ridge and sound comes around the sides of the tongue. Singers like to vocalize on "la-la-la" because only the tip of the tongue is involved. If the [l] is incorrectly curled back along the hard palate, the vowels before and after it are darkened. Correct this by singing "lee-lee-lee" with the tongue pointed forward.

Sometimes a vowel before an [l] is spoiled if the tongue rises too soon or too slowly toward the [l] position. After a vowel, make [l] as quickly and as late as possible.

23. [h], *Aitch*, is the friction of air passing through the open mouth. Let the friction occur at a place that is high and forward on the roof of the mouth, as it naturally is in the name "Hugh." [h] is a quiet consonant that needs extra energy in a large room.

24. [hw], *Which*, is a sound of friction as air passes through lips shaped for [u]. We do not hear the [u] because the lips move quickly to the position of the following vowel. The double symbol, [hw], shows that the sound is frictional, like [h], and also involves a quick glide, like [hw].

# R: the variable sound

We learned in chapter 6 about the vowel [ɜ], which always has the consonant letter R in its spelling. This is just one of many sounds that we associate with R.

When R is followed by a vowel, it works as a consonant and must be pronounced. This is true when R and the following vowel are in the same word, as in "rose," and also when they are in different words, as in "far away."

There are two correct ways to pronounce [r] in singing English:

(1) *English R* [r], pronounced with the tongue forward, not pulled back or tense. The lips may be rounded. Some experts analyze [r] as a glide, produced by moving from the sound of [ɜ] to another vowel sound.

(2) *Flipped R* [ɾ], if you are using a formal or British style and if the R is between two vowels. To discover this sound, say "veddy meddy" several times quickly, lightening the *dd* until you are saying "very merry."

Caution: Do not *roll* [r]. Rolled R is not part of Standard American.

What if R is followed by a consonant or by a silence? Minimize the Ahr and keep the preceding vowel as relaxed as possible. Sometimes you might omit Ahr completely, so that "lark" is pronounced "lahk." At other times you may sing a schwa instead of Ahr; chapter 8 will tell more about this substitution.

Sometimes a vowel before Ahr is spoiled if the tongue rises too soon or too slowly toward the Ahr position. This is such a common fault that almost every voice student has to work on it.

In summary, for Standard American diction you need two kinds of R: American and Flipped. For other European languages you also need two kinds of R: Rolled and Flipped.

# Clusters and legato singing

Our language is rich in consonants. Think of an ordinary sentence like "This plant sprouts from seeds," which has five vowels and seventeen consonant sounds. Between the vowel in "plant" and the vowel in "sprouts" there are five consecutive consonants, three of which are unvoiced. No wonder it is difficult to sing smoothly in English!

Some singers become so intent on singing smoothly—the Italian word is *legato*—that they leave out consonants altogether or they articulate them weakly and flood them out with a stream of vowels. Such singing leaves no gap in the sound but unfortunate gaps in the meaning of the words. Listeners catch a bit of a word here and there and struggle to hear what the song is about. They are likely to go home saying, "I don't like to hear singers much. You can never understand them." We do not want that to happen!

No book can give separate exercises for all of the thousands of combinations of two, three, four, and five consonants that occur in English. We can, however, work for clarity and agility with tongue twisters and rapid speech patterns.

There are two common problems in diction: weakness, or lack of clarity, and choppiness, or lack of smooth connections. Here are ways to work on your songs and overcome these problems.

If your consonants are too weak, try whispering the words of your song loudly enough so that your whisper can be heard across the room. Notice the energy level that vigorous articulation requires and then use this level in your singing. Loud whispering is fairly strenuous; do it only for short periods of time.

If your diction is choppy, try chanting, or singing the song text on a single pitch. At first, let the timing be free so that you can concentrate on the clarity of the vowels and consonants. Pay special attention to the way one word connects to another. Let the final consonant of one word connect with the beginning of the next word, unless your ear tells you that the words have to be separated to make sense. When your chanting is smooth, try doing it in the correct rhythm of the song. Let the legato you have developed carry over into your singing.

## Speaking exercises

Speak these words in a galloping singsong rhythm, quickly and lightly. Let the speed increase until you can speak all four lines in one breath. Purpose: to sensitize the main articulators and develop agility.

> The lips, the teeth, the tip of the tongue,
> the lips, the teeth, the tip of the tongue,
> the lips, the teeth, the tip of the tongue,
> the tip of the, tip of the, tip of the tongue!

Tongue twisters and many poems make excellent articulation drills. Learn to speak the following rapidly and clearly, and then sing them on comfortable middle to low pitches.

> A tutor who tooted a flute
> Once tutored two tooters to toot.
>    Said the two to the tutor
>    "Is it harder to toot,
> Or to tutor two tooters to toot?"

> Peter Piper picked a peck of pickled peppers. A peck of pickled peppers Peter Piper picked. If Peter Piper picked a peck of pickled peppers, where's the peck of pickled peppers Peter Piper picked?

> Blow, bugle, blow, set the wild echoes flying,
> Blow, bugle; answer, echoes, dying, dying, dying.
>    —Alfred Lord Tennyson, from "The Princess"

> Boot, saddle, to horse, and away!
> Rescue my castle before the hot day
> Brightens to blue from its silvery gray.
> Boot, saddle, to horse, and away!
>    —Robert Browning, from "Boot and Saddle"

Because of its meaning, the following poem must be spoken slowly but with perfectly precise articulation.

> I stepped from plank to plank
> A slow and cautious way;
> The stars about my head I felt,
> About my feet the sea.
>
> I knew not but the next
>   Would be my final inch,
> This gave me that precarious gait
>   Some call experience.
> —Emily Dickinson

## Singing exercises

**7.1** **La-Beh-Da.** Sing these syllables one measure at a time until you are used to them, then let the speed increase until you can sing all three measures in one breath. (These syllables alternate lip and tongue consonants. They have been used by singers since the 1700s.) Purpose: to develop articulatory agility on a musical pattern.

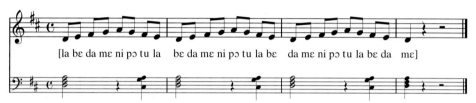

[la bɛ da mɛ ni pɔ tu la    bɛ da mɛ ni pɔ tu la bɛ    da mɛ ni pɔ tu la bɛ da    mɛ]

**7.2** **Connections.** Use these words to test yourself on some of the common problems mentioned in the chapter. Purpose: to exercise consonant connections and consonants that are often misused.

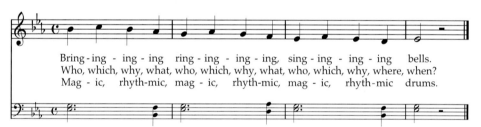

Bring - ing - ing - ing    ring - ing - ing - ing,    sing - ing - ing - ing    bells.
Who, which, why, what, who, which, why, what, who, which, why, where, when?
Mag - ic,    rhyth-mic,    mag - ic,    rhyth-mic,    mag - ic,    rhyth-mic    drums.

**7.3** **Yah-Yah.** Sing this pattern with many different consonants and vowels. Be sure that voiced consonants begin on pitch and that the lowest note is in tune. This works well with a teacher or student leading and the class echoing back. Purpose: to assure that all vowels, semivowels, and voiced and unvoiced consonants can be sung both high and low in the voice.

ja    ja    ja    ja        ja    ja    ja    ja
wi    wi    wi    wi        wi    wi    wi    wi
zɔ    zɔ    zɔ    zɔ        zɔ    zɔ    zɔ    zɔ
blu   blu   blu   blu       blu   blu   blu   blu

## Additional reading

*Audiocassettes with examples spoken by both a female and a male trained speaker accompany this thorough book, which is especially recommended if you would like to lose an accent:*
*American Diction for Singers* by Geoffrey G. Forward. Vocal Power Institute, 9826 Columbus Avenue, North Hills, CA 91343.

# 8 Double and Triple Vowels

*Guiding questions:* *How does one sing syllables with more than one vowel? What about final r?*

WHEN words are slowed down by singing them, we discover surprising things about spelling and pronunciation. The same letter can stand for various different sounds, and some vowels are difficult to tell apart. Also, some common sounds that we learned as vowels are not single vowels at all but combinations of two or three vowels.

In chapter 6 we noticed that Ay and Oh, when they are spoken slowly, consist of combinations of vowel sounds. Such combinations are called *diphthongs* and *triphthongs*, Greek words that mean "double sounds" and "triple sounds." (Pronounce the "ph" carefully as [f] in both "dif-thong" and "trif-thong".)

Most languages spell out diphthongs clearly with one letter for each vowel. English spelling sneaks diphthongs in without showing them: the phrase "I go" appears to have two vowels in it, but actually it has two diphthongs, adding up to four vowels. Some people become frustrated with such problems and say that the English language has no pure vowels, but that is not true either.

As singers, we know that our words will be prolonged by music and that every detail of our pronunciation will be noticeable to our audience. How will we sing "I go" if the music makes each syllable last for several seconds?

## Five diphthongs

All English diphthongs follow this pattern: *the first vowel is stronger and more open, and the second vowel is weaker and more closed.* (If the weaker vowel comes first, we call it a glide semiconsonant, as in the syllables [ju] or [wi].)

The strong/weak vowel pattern leads to our main rule for singing diphthongs: *stay on the stronger vowel as long as possible and sing the weaker vowel as late and as quickly as possible.* Some speech teachers use the term "vanish vowel" to describe the weak vowel of a diphthong.

The key to singing diphthongs well is knowing exactly what vowel sounds you wish to sing. Some of us speak local dialects that close the vowels more than necessary; our singing will be more comfortable and pleasant with correct standard American diphthongs.

These are the five main diphthongs. Each one can be identified by the numbers of the two vowels that make it up. (The numbers come from Appendix B, page 272.)

| IPA symbol: | English name: | Some possible spellings: |
|---|---|---|
| 4+2. [ɛɪ] | Long Ay | late, may, raise, weigh |
| 6+2. [aɪ] | Long I | I, pie, my, aisle |
| 9+2. [ɔɪ] | Oy | toy, noise |
| 6+11. [aʊ] | Ow | how, house |
| 10+11. [oʊ] | Long Oh | so, low, moan |

4+2. [ɛɪ], *Long Ay,* is usually described as a combination of vowels 3+1, [eɪ]. In singing, this combination turns out to be too tense for comfort, and it is often misunderstood as [i]. The sound is better and clearer if we use 4+2, [ɛɪ], prolonging [ɛ] as the main vowel. In order to relax this sound and clarify it in your mind practice "late" and other *Ay* words as shown in exercise 8.1. This pronunciation may seem peculiar in speaking, but it will be just right when you sing it.

6+2. [aɪ], *Long I,* consists of Bright Ah and Short I in standard American, producing a clear but relaxed pronunciation. For a country-western sound, try changing the second vowel to [i] and spend extra time on it.

9+2. [ɔɪ], *Oy,* uses Open Oh and Short I. Even if your local dialect does not use Open Oh alone, you probably use it in this diphthong.

6+11. [aʊ], *Ow,* consists of Bright Ah and Short U. Just as [i] is too closed for good singing of diphthongs, so is [u], and we use [ʊ] instead for the vanish vowel.

10+11. [oʊ], *Long Oh,* consists of Pure Oh and Short U. Be sure that the first vowel is a clear Oh; some British dialects use a mixed vowel much like #15, [ɜ], with no Oh quality at all.

# Schwa-diphthongs

We learned in chapter 7 that [r] causes problems if it involves too much tension in the tongue. For greater relaxation, or for very formal English, you may drop *r* completely before another consonant or before a silence. If you do so, you will discover some words in which you can replace [r] with [ə].

Here is an example: "or." In daily speech most Americans say a vowel plus a consonant, [ɔr]. If you want to avoid American *r* and its tongue tension, you can say [ɔə]. It will sound formal, but clear and relaxed. To sound less formal, you can put some [r]-coloring into the schwa, saying [ɔɚ]: the tag on the schwa shows that [r]-coloring is heard, but it does not completely cover up the vowel quality of the schwa.

There are five such diphthongs in which a schwa replaces a final *r* or *re.* All five can be spoken with or without [r]-coloring. Because [r]-coloring is normal and correct in Standard American, we show it in IPA by adding a tag to the schwa.

Remember to relax your tongue when practicing schwa-diphthongs.

| IPA Symbol: | English name: | Some possible spellings: |
|---|---|---|
| 2+14. [ɪɚ] | Ear-diphthong | beer, bier, shear, we're, merely |
| 4+14. [ɛɚ] | Air-diphthong | bear, there, their, e'er, careful |
| 7+14. [ɑɚ] | Are-diphthong | far, art, barge, sergeant |
| 9+14. [ɔɚ] | Or-diphthong | shore, soar, your, door, o'er |
| 11+14. [ʊɚ] | Tour-diphthong | cure, poor, your, you're |

Practice these diphthongs just as you do the five main diphthongs. Make the first vowel sound clear, even if the spelling looks confusing. You can try more or less [r]-coloring, from none at all to a country twang.

Keep in mind that schwa-diphthongs occur only at times when *r* can be omitted, that is, before a consonant or before a silence (for instance, when you take a breath). If *r* comes before a vowel, the consonant [r] must be pronounced, and there is no schwa-diphthong. Some examples:

- hear it [hɪrɪt]
- swear it [swɛrɪt]
- pour it [pɔrɪt]
- assure it [əʃʊrɪt]

- hereafter [hɪræftɚ]
- wherever [hwɛrɛvɚ]
- forever [fɔrɛvɚ]
- curable [kjʊrəbəl]

## Schwa-triphthongs

If a final [r] sound comes after a diphthong, changing [r] to a schwa results in a triphthong. After practicing the schwa-diphthongs you will have no trouble with these sounds.

| IPA symbol: | English name: | Some possible spellings: |
|---|---|---|
| 6+2+14. [aɪə] | Ire-triphthong | fire, briar, lyre, choir |
| 6+11+14. [aʊə] | Our-triphthong | sour, flower |

In both triphthongs [a] is prolonged in singing; the two weaker vowels come quickly and lightly at the end. Again, if the next sound is a vowel, the *r* must be pronounced, and there is no schwa.

Our goal in learning about schwa-diphthongs and schwa-triphthongs was to reduce the amount of tongue tension associated with the consonant *r*. We often think that formality means stiffness, but in this case formal speech brings relaxation and ease in using the tongue.

## Exercises

**8.1  Diphthongs.** Practice this pattern with many different words that contain diphthongs. These words are written in IPA; what are they? Purpose: to identify the vowels that must be lengthened in the five main diphthongs.

**8.2  Diphthong and Triphthong Slurs.** Purpose: to identify the components of the schwa-diphthongs.

# 9 Performing a Song

*Guiding questions:*   *How can I get the most feeling out of a song—is there a "right way," or can I do it all my own way? What is "style"? How can I keep a song interesting from beginning to end? What is the role of my accompanist? How can I get over stage fright? How should I behave on stage, and how can I get the meaning of a song across to an audience?*

YOU have been learning about the technique of singing: how your voice works and how to sing so that your voice sounds its best and does what you want it to do. It is time now to sing songs, while you go on learning.

Should you wait to sing songs until your voice is "perfect"? No. In fact, your vocal technique will develop more quickly if you combine working on technique and working on songs. You will draw inspiration from the emotional energy of a song you love. Also, your voice learns to work comfortably and reliably when you sing the same music many times, if you just stay alert to your goals of beautiful tone and physical ease.

The goal of all your work is to reach the point of singing songs for others. When that time comes, you must be able to focus on the music and trust that the good vocal habits you have practiced will keep you singing well.

## Guidelines for interpretation

Notes printed on a page—we call them music, but there really is no music until we make the sounds that they stand for. When we go beyond making the right sounds and communicate the message that was in the mind of the person who composed the music, then we can say that we are "interpreting" the music. Interpretation means dealing with the psychological and aesthetic areas of music. Here are some basic principles to guide the process of interpretation.

*The words come first.* Words are written before music nearly always. The composer takes the feelings in the words and puts them into music. We rediscover those feelings and let them guide our singing. To interpret a song well, we have to understand the words and feel good about putting them across to other people. The words determine many things about how we perform, including when we breathe and what facial expression we have. Everything we do must fit the words and never go against them.

*Rhythm is the heartbeat of music*, as we all know from intuition and experience. If the rhythm is weak or unsteady, so is the music. Even though we know this, we sometimes become so concerned about tone quality and other aspects of music that we let the rhythm waver or stop altogether.

There are two rhythmic principles that will keep you from "losing the beat." First, *the rhythm starts with the first note of music and continues until the last note dies away.* If there is a piano introduction, start singing mentally with the first note you hear. If there are rests in the song, sing through them mentally, and do the same with a postlude after the song. If your mind wanders during the music, the people who are listening may not know why, but their minds will wander, too. When you are not singing, simply listen to the piano and enjoy the music. Your enjoyment will show, and the audience will pay attention, too.

Also, *you may hurry or slow down any note of music at any time for any interpretive reason.* You have complete freedom—and complete responsibility. The basic beat of the music, the tempo, may quicken in order to express excitement. Much more often, the tempo slows down in order to focus expression on a certain note or series of notes or to express some degree of relaxation or satisfaction or some other feeling. No rule tells us exactly when and how much to vary tempos; our imaginations must tell us.

Because music is an art, no one can say that a song must be performed in a certain way and no other way. The personal feelings and viewpoint that you bring to the words and music will be appreciated. On the other hand, we want to know that your way of doing a song is true to the composer's ideas. If this is not the case, we may ask why you chose to sing that song instead of some other song that fits your taste better. All of this brings us to the subject of musical styles.

*Musical styles*

"Style" means many things in musical performance. Here are some of the ways musicians talk about style. Try to relate these to actual pieces of music and singers you have heard. Style can mean the following:

1.  A type of music: classical music in contrast to pop music, rhythm and blues in contrast to country.

2.  A historical period: Classical music in contrast to Baroque music, which came before it, and Romantic music, which came after it.

3.  A manner of expression: dramatic in contrast to lyrical.

4.  A way of performing that we associate with a specific composer or school of composers, such as Mozart style or Russian style.

5.  A way of performing that belongs to an individual. Your personal style includes your individual vocal quality and your tendency to do certain things well, as well as the projection of your personality. When you develop your personal style, you learn to eliminate sounds that imitate other singers and use sounds that are yours alone.

How do you learn about style? By listening thoughtfully to many kinds of music, done by many kinds of performers. Reading about music and musicians will help you build a vocabulary and define your ideas about styles. Through listening, reading, discussion, and experimentation you will learn what musical styles you like best, what styles you most want to perform, and how to develop a personal style.

*Beginning, middle, and end*

Because we cannot see music and because it goes by us in time, we often talk about it in words that describe shapes, using expressions like "the rise and fall of melody," "thin and thick textures," or "symmetrical form."

In general, the word "form" describes patterns of repetition or nonrepetition in music. Understanding the form of a song makes it easier to memorize. More important, awareness of musical form helps you to perform better. If we understand the form ourselves, we can help the audience to know when a song repeats, where the climax is, and when the end is coming.

*Strophic songs*

Many songs are written in *stanzas,* or verses, which use the same music two or more times to different words. Such songs are called *strophic,* a word derived from Greek for "a turning," because a singer would usually turn from one side of the audience to the other at the end of a stanza (still a good idea!). A good melody is worth hearing more than once, and the audience will remain interested if we keep the words interesting. The last stanza might need something special to give it a sense of climax and completeness. Try a slight delay in starting the final stanza or a surge of extra energy or even a slight change in tempo. Near the end you might hold out a particular note or stretch out a phrase for extra expression.

**Through-composed songs**

If the composer wrote new music for two or more parts of the poem, a song is said to be *through-composed*, even if it includes some pattern of repetition. One common pattern is called "three-part song form," in which there are two stanzas of music separated by a contrasting stanza.

**Pop-song form**

Many popular and Broadway songs follow *pop-song form*. After an introductory *verse*, the *chorus* begins with an eight-measure melody, called "the 1st 8." This is repeated with new words as "the 2nd 8." For contrast, a new eight-measure melody follows, called the "bridge" or "release." Then the first melody comes back in the "return." "Ain't Misbehavin'" is a good example of pop-song form.

- mm. 1–8 Introduction
- mm. 9–24 Verse (background reasons for the song)
- mm. 25–32 1st 8
- mm. 33–40 2nd 8
- mm. 41–48 Bridge
- mm. 49–56 Return

"A Cockeyed Optimist" also has pop-song form, but the main sections of the song are each sixteen measures long rather than eight. To create a strong climax, the return lasts an extra eight measures ("not this heart"). In pop music an extra ending is called a "tag," in classical music, a *coda*. Which other songs in this book have pop-song form? Which have tags?

Whether you are singing Broadway or classical songs, you can help your audience enjoy your song more if you make the form clear in your performance. Here are some ways:

- Allow some extra time, even a silence, between the verse and the chorus.
- Change your delivery in some way to call attention to the contrasting section or bridge; perhaps this is the time to move or change your posture.
- Slow down a little at the end of the bridge so that the return brings back the first tempo along with the melody.

These are suggestions; not every one will work in every song. Whatever song you sing, decide where its climax is. Plan how you will build toward the climax and how you will relax the energy of the song afterward.

**The accompanist**

Every thinking singer knows that the piano accompanist is a Very Important Person. A good accompanist can make you sing better than you ever thought you could. A poor one can make you sound as if you never practiced at all. A friendly accompanist makes it easy and pleasant for you to perform, but a thoughtless accompanist can drown you out and distract the audience from your performance. So find the best accompanist you can and treat that person well.

*Give your accompanist good sheet music to play from.* I have seen someone walk into an audition, hand the pianist a folded, gray (illegal) photocopy and say, "I sing this down from where it's written." Such behavior shows ignorance and poor planning. If the accompanist cannot read the music and plays wrong notes, it is your performance that suffers.

*Give your accompanist enough time to learn the music.* Choose your music and give it to the accompanist well ahead of the due date.

Some pianists can transpose (play a song in a different key from the written one), and some cannot; few pianists are willing to transpose at sight. Transposing is a complex skill that not every musician develops.

*Take rehearsals seriously.* Prepare your music and arrive on time, ready to work. Rehearsals help each of you to understand how best to help the other. *Let your pianist express opinions* both about the music and about your singing. You can learn a lot from an experienced pianist. If you are singing out of tune or have learned a wrong note, it is certainly better to let the pianist say so than to continue making the error.

*Be sure your accompanist feels well paid,* whether in money or in appreciation or both.

## Confidence and stage fright

By singing regularly for your voice teacher and other voice students, you have gone a long way toward feeling comfortable about public performance.

Even so, it is natural to want to do your best in front of others. For some singers this natural desire to do well takes the exaggerated form of "stage fright" and gets in the way of their real goal of communication. Let's learn to minimize stage fright so that we enjoy the excitement of performing without the negative effects of fear.

Confidence lies in knowing that you can do well and that your listeners will like what you offer them. After all, you are gracious in recognizing the good in other singers' performances, and you should recognize the good in your own.

Some of us remember other persons in our past who judged us negatively (or we thought they did). It may be necessary to do some mental work to deal with those "internal judges." Here is one approach: Imagine your judges sitting in the audience while you perform, and picture smiles on their faces. (If those persons, in fact, cannot express any pleasant feelings, that is their problem.)

Should you not criticize yourself? Yes, in the practice room or in class, but *not at all onstage.*

Learn to criticize yourself objectively. Objective self-criticism sounds like this: "I forgot a word in the second verse, and I think I sang flat in the last phrase." Objective self-criticism says that you want to improve and gives others a chance to help you by agreeing or disagreeing with your evaluation of your performance.

Subjective self-criticism, complaining, sounds like: "I was awful, and I blew the whole thing!" Such criticism gets in the way of improvement and keeps you from thinking about specific ways to do better. Subjective self-criticism is tiresome to other people because it is self-centered. It shuts the door to comments from others. (If you say you sang terribly, then anyone who says otherwise must be ignorant or insincere or both.) Learn to thank others for their positive comments and to invite their suggestions for improvement.

The essential ingredient to confidence is preparation. As part of your daily practice, think of preparing for a performance: Can you sing well after eating? How much warm-up do you need? Can you sing your song acceptably every day or only on rare occasions when you feel especially good?

If you can sing your songs well every day for a week before the performance, then you need have no fear about singing them on the performance day, too. If a song is not reliable for you on a daily basis, then keep it in the practice room and put a more comfortable song in front of the public.

## Preparations

As a performance approaches, learn what you can about the audience for whom you will sing. Visit the place and practice on the stage where you will perform, if possible. Plan how you will enter and where you will stand. Plan what you will wear and be sure that the neckline and waistline feel comfortable when you breathe.

Plan what you will say: Will you welcome the audience? Will you introduce yourself and your accompanist? Will you introduce your songs? Do you know how to pronounce the titles and composers of your songs? Being prepared is the key to confidence.

A special note to college students and to singers who enter competitions: you may be singing before a committee of voice teachers. Rather than being a tough, supercritical audience, voice teachers are the most sympathetic listeners you could have. They have heard many beginners, and they know the pitfalls of singing. Voice teachers are intensely interested in voices, otherwise they would not be in their profession, and they sincerely want you to succeed. Sing to them as you would to an audience of friends. Forgive them if their unpleasant duty of writing criticisms and giving grades sometimes causes them to forget their best selves.

## Onstage

After all of your preparations are done, performance onstage is a natural climax to a pleasant process. One of the best mental attitudes to maintain is that the stage is your home, that the members of the audience are your guests at a party, and that the music is entertainment (even the food) that you are offering to them. This little game of the imagination takes your attention away from yourself and focuses it on making sure that your listeners have a good time.

Performances of classical music are somewhat formal, but only because we want everyone to enjoy the music without any distraction or annoyance. Too much formality looks stiff and unfriendly; too much casualness looks disorganized and careless. Stage etiquette does not mean following a list of rules; it simply means doing things smoothly and without fuss.

The singer enters the stage first, followed by the accompanist and the page turner, if any. Walk to your place at a normal rate. Avoid crossing in front of someone else, and avoid turning your back to the audience. If the audience welcomes you with applause, bow slightly to thank them. Simply lean forward enough to take a good look at your shoes; that is a bow.

If there is no printed program, you need to say hello to the audience and introduce yourself and your accompanist. Speak clearly, audibly, and slowly enough so that everyone can understand you. In addition to saying the name of your song and its composer, you may want to tell the audience something of interest about your song. People feel that they know you better if you talk, as well as sing to them, and you may find that their positive acceptance of what you say puts you more at ease.

If your song is in a foreign language, be sure that you give a summary of what it is about, either orally or in the printed program. It is impolite to confront your guests in a foreign language without explaining it.

When you are ready to sing, be sure that the first words of the song are in your mind. Take a good breath and let it out again silently, making sure that your breathing muscles are not stiff.

You may signal to the accompanist to begin the song, or you may let the accompanist sense when you are ready; agree beforehand on a preference. From the first note of the introduction, you are already in the mood of the song.

If your song has no piano introduction, ask your pianist to play your starting note quietly as the top note of the first chord of the song.

"Well begun is half done," says a wise proverb. Give full attention to the first notes you sing, making sure you give them enough time and enough energy to be heard clearly. Once the song is launched on its way, give your attention to the meaning of the words and what you want to say to the audience. Keep thinking ahead, so that when you end a phrase, the next phrase is already fully formed in your imagination.

"The eyes are the windows of the soul," says another proverb. Your listeners want more than just to hear your voice—they want you to communicate with them personally. In two or three minutes you can direct some of your song to every part of the audience. If you think that seeing faces may disturb you, try focusing on a point just between two persons' heads. Singing with your eyes either closed or raised to the ceiling is not a good practice; people quickly see that you are singing "over their heads" and their minds will tend to wander.

Keep the mood of the song through piano interludes, through all of your own singing (whether you are pleased with it or not), and through the ending of the song until the last note stops sounding.

May you use gestures? Yes, if they come easily. Pointless arm waving detracts from the music, but unnatural stiffness detracts as well. Let the music and words tell you what to do; a gesture that flows naturally from the meaning of the song will enhance your performance.

What about mishaps? Stay in the mood of the song. Think ahead to the next phrase on which you and the pianist can get together and go on. Most mishaps go by without the audience knowing or caring; they still enjoy the song if you go on performing without giving off distress signals. If a singer is in trouble, it is not a good idea to flash a glance at the accompanist; the glance advertises the problem and looks like an attempt to put blame on the innocent pianist.

When the music ends and you let go of your concentration, the audience knows the song is over. Bow again modestly, just as you did before; a bow says, "Thank you for listening to me." After acknowledging the audience, smile at the accompanist, again to say, "Thank you." After a group of several songs or after a particularly difficult piece, gesture to your accompanist to stand and take a bow with you. Then you both leave the stage together, usually in the order in which you entered the stage.

Courtesy in performance means that you put the audience's pleasure and comfort ahead of your own. If you do not feel well, you decide (with your teacher) whether to sing or not; but you do not worry the audience by making an apology about being sick. An apology makes people fear that you are hurting yourself, and maybe even your voice, on their account. Also, be courteous after a performance, even if you are disappointed with your own singing. Anyone who has enjoyed your singing deserves to receive your thanks, not your disgust over slight mishaps.

*Additional reading*

*For insight into style and interpretation in classical music, read the song analyses in:*
*The Art of Accompanying by Robert Spillman. Schirmer Books, New York, 1985.*

*More important than any reading: your own attendance at events when others perform. Observe*
*thoughtfully and learn.*

# 10 Extending Your Voice

*Guiding questions:*

*How can I go on building my voice to make it stronger? How can I develop my breath control and sing longer phrases? How can I learn to sing quick patterns, like scales and ornaments? How can I sing better low notes and better high notes?*

YOUR vocal exercises until now have focused on the middle range, where most singing is done. When you and your teacher agree that this essential core sounds and feels right, it is time to move on to other challenges.

When you work on your voice, use a balance of ambition and patience. Reach a little beyond what you can do now, so that your voice will grow. Keep an open attitude if your teacher asks you to try something new. But vocal growth cannot be forced by overworking the voice. If you ever hear hoarseness or feel pain, stop and rest a few minutes and change the exercise.

## Vocal strength

The voice is not a muscle that grows stronger in proportion to exercise. The voice gains in power and stamina by becoming more efficient, more effective in resonating the sound that comes from the vocal cords. Your singing will benefit from improved general fitness, but the tiny muscles that actually produce the voice are strong enough for singing in almost everyone.

A physician who examines your vocal cords will not see much, if any, change in them as a result of vocal study. But their way of working changes according to your mental concepts. As you imagine a desired tone quality, the vocal cords and resonators adjust to reproduce the imagined sound as nearly as they can. Repeated practice brings finer tuning, producing the results you want more perfectly and easily.

Because your imagination guides the whole process of vocal growth, you must be aware and alert during practice. If you try to strengthen your voice by singing scales while you read a newspaper, you will only train bad habits and hurt your voice.

In chapter 4 we said, "Let your feelings be the key to vocal resonance." Your will to communicate with others is still the best motivation to increase your vocal resonance.

### Focus

*Mental focus* aims to direct the voice toward a goal. When you throw a ball at a target, you think about the target and not about the way your arm moves. Just as your brain tells your arm how to throw, it will tell your vocal muscles how to make a tone reach listeners at the back of an auditorium. Your breath does not blow the voice across the room; rather, your voice causes sound waves that travel across a distance.

Mental focus works in other ways, also. Some singers improve their vocal cord function by *visualizing* the smooth, complete contact of the vocal cords as if watching them on a screen.

**Figure 10.1**

Many singers also use mental focus in the form called *voice placement*. Most good singers feel concentrated vibrations that accompany their best tones. By recalling the vibrating sensations, singers learn to reproduce the good singing that caused them.

Steady breath supply is a prerequisite for focused tone, and often a weak tone can be reinforced by improving the breath supply. Singing on sustained, buzzing consonants is an excellent way to assure that the breath supply is steady and energetic. Especially good are the voiced consonants [z] and [ʒ], which direct air through a narrow channel toward the front teeth.

A technique that often helps to increase resonance is this: with your thumbs resting on each side of your jaw, let the tips of your longest fingers meet in front of the bridge of your nose. This forms a little "porch" in front of your face; keep your elbows down and arms relaxed so that the porch is not too wide. When you sing into the "porch," you will feel more willing to let the tone go free. When you take your hands away, try to achieve the same sensations of vocal freedom (Figure 10.1).

## Improving breath control

Breath control improves when vocal tone becomes more concentrated. Good tone is efficient; that is, maximum resonance is produced with a minimum amount of air. After the first few lessons it may be unnecessary to say much about breathing because good breath support will occur automatically when tonal concepts are correct.

If your breathing does not respond automatically to the demands you make, review the lessons learned in chapter 3:

- Do your lower ribs expand, including the lower back?
- Do the abdominal muscles relax outward to let breath flow in?
- Do the lower ribs remain expanded when you begin to sing?
- Do you support the singing tone with energized abdominal muscles?

Centuries ago, singers discovered a test for efficient tone production: Hold a lighted candle a few inches in front of your open mouth while you sing a vowel.

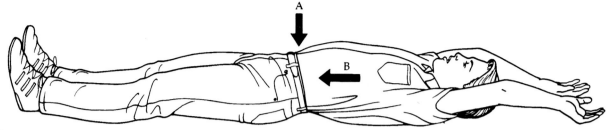

**Figure 10.2**

*If you sing lying down, gravity (A) draws your abdomen toward the floor. Your diaphragm, pushing in the direction of arrow B, resists the fall of the abdominal organs and prevents them from pushing the air out of your body too fast.*

If the candle flickers, too much air is escaping. Try it. When you can vocalize without making the candle flame waver, you will understand that good singing takes much less air than one would think.

"Drink the tone in" is an example of a mental concept that singers use to economize their breath. Even though air is leaving the body, the thought of air coming into the body slows the rate of movement.

As the abdominal muscles move in to support the breath, the diaphragm resists them, slowing down their motion. You can sense this by singing while lying down on the floor. Use a thin book to pillow your head, and sing as normally as possible (Figure 10.2).

Another trick singers use is to wear an elastic belt that pulls in the abdomen. Instead of pulling the abdomen in more quickly, the belt energizes the muscles to resist collapse. Sporting-goods stores sell an elastic "tummy trimmer" to be worn while exercising. It is about seven inches wide and is fastened with Velcro so that it fits anyone.

## Flexibility

Many styles of music require flexibility, or the ability to sing notes rapidly. Not only opera singers need flexibility; folk and gospel singers also use quick flourishes of notes that one must practice to acquire. In some musical styles a singer sings only the written notes, but other styles allow freedom to improvise and add ornaments at will.

Certain standardized "ornaments" have been compared to the compulsory figures practiced by ice skaters. The most basic ornament is alternation between a melody note and the note above it, called the "upper neighbor." Exercise 10.1 shows an example of an upper neighbor (UN) and some common variations based on it. As with other forms of vocal exercise, the main ingredient is your musical imagination. If you can form a quick ornament clearly in your mind, your brain will tell your voice how to sing it.

## Exercise

10.1  **Upper Neighbors.** Try these patterns, which can be used in various styles of music. Purpose: to make the voice flexible.

# Range

I have never yet met a student who had a small vocal range, but I have known many who limited themselves to a small range. They felt unsure of new sensations and unfamiliar tones. They needed confidence and guidance to learn to accept their full vocal range.

Your voice almost certainly has a range of two octaves or more (unless there is a problem that deserves therapy, such as nodules). Your full range probably extends to three octaves, if you include the lightest high tones, falsetto in men and "whistle tones" in women (which seem useless for singing but play an important role in extending your range), and the lowest tones (even the soft breathy ones below the normal chest tones).

How much of your range can you use for singing songs? The answer depends on

- the amount of freedom your vocal mechanism has when it adjusts to register changes;
- the musical styles you prefer to sing and whether they use a wide range; and
- your personal willingness to accept the sounds that are natural to various registers of your voice.

## *Low notes*

If you speak at a pitch near the lower end of your vocal range, your low notes probably already feel strong. If this is the case, you may find that vocal study changes your lower voice much less than it changes your upper voice.

To reach the maximum power of your low notes, you may need no more than a few reminders to focus and use your tonal energy. (Even a natural bass may feel shy about using the strong low notes that are his special gift.) Often, however, young women hesitate to use chest tones, feeling that they are ugly or unmusical.

One way to discover how much energy the chest voice needs is to speak the words of a song vigorously and then to concentrate on the same physical sensations while singing the same words.

Another way to learn about the chest voice is to use a deliberately ugly, "brassy" sound in the syllable "quack."

# Exercises

**10.2 Quack-quack.** Use lots of energy. There is no way to make this sound beautiful, so have fun with it. Move your jaw, lips, and tongue freely, without tension. Transpose the pattern to several different keys in the lower part of your range. Practice this for only a few minutes at a time.

When you vocalize to strengthen the resonance of low notes, it is important to use a bright tone quality and good posture. Lowering your head does not help, it merely restricts the freedom of the throat.

[kwæ kwæ kwæ kwæ kwæ kwæ kwæ kwæ kwæk]

**10.3  Low Scale and Turn.** Look straight ahead and keep your posture. Sing very legato and drop the jaw well. After the four-note scale, observe the rest, but do not take breath; sing the *turn* on the same breath. Purpose: to focus resonance for the lowest tones.

[i    a    i    a    a _____          i   a i  a    a _____ ]

*High notes*

High notes develop more noticeably than low notes for many students simply because the high voice has not been used much and it responds quickly to encouragement. If your low notes seem to become weaker as you develop the highs, this is an illusion. The low voice simply has less growing to do.

If high tones come easily to you, accept the gift with thanks and use it with pleasure. They require more time and practice for some people because of the fine adjustment needed between breath energy and precise function of the vocal cords.

One biological function of the vocal cords is to close tightly when the breath is put under pressure, as in lifting a heavy weight. When the vocal cords sense high air pressure, a reflex closes them tightly to hold it back. A singer has to overcome this natural reflex so that the vocal cords gently close the right amount for singing; they must not clutch and stop the airflow entirely.

Upper tones can be found gently with exercises 1.6 through 1.8. Start without a pitch from the piano; sing a high pitch first, then find out what it was. You are singing spontaneously, instead of trying to force the voice to sing tones that it may not be ready for. Now vocalize downward a few times. When you repeat this process, you may find that the voice has warmed up and is ready for a somewhat higher note. You can also do this with any of the hum-consonants or with the "Bubble" used in exercise 2.6.

If you start an exercise in a low key and move it up gradually, go only as high as you can sing with a feeling of freedom and ease in your throat. If your throat tightens, rest for at least a few seconds and then start over with a different exercise.

Consider this quotation from a voice teacher of long experience, Oren Brown of New York City: "Take only what the voice gives you." And here is another that he has said often: "Think the tone and let it happen."

A successful way to discover and practice high notes is the "Open-mouth Hum," described by another prominent voice teacher, the late Dr. Berton Coffin. It resembles an [m]-hum, but without the disadvantage of having the mouth closed.

**10.4  Open-Mouth Hum.** Sing [a], but cover your mouth completely either with the palm of your hand or with the back of your hand. No air escapes from your mouth; the air and the tone pass through your nose instead. Repeat the phrase with your mouth open. Purpose: to discover a light, free approach to higher notes.

Singing "behind the hand" can be used to practice any vowel and any musical phrase. It has helped many women to discover the "whistle" tones on "High C" and above. These tones are very small at first, but they may develop to usable strength.

**Exercises**

(Open-mouth hum)                    [a _____ ]

**10.5  Two-Octave Scale.** Sing very softly on [i] or any vowel that is easy for you. If the voice breaks or skips notes as the register changes, start again more softly. Find at least one starting tone on which you can do this long scale easily. Purpose: to learn to pass through register changes smoothly.

[i _____ ]

**10.6  Three Scales—3 + 5 + 9.** Sing the three scales separately at first. Later, combine them into one long phrase. Practice at various volume levels, not always loud or always soft. Purpose: to exercise the voice quickly and lightly through a wider range while building flexibility.

[i __ a __ i _____ a _____ i __ a _____ ]

**10.7  Legato Chords.** Sing very smoothly. Feel a special continuity between the contrasting vowels [i] and [ɔ]. Close [ɔ] to [o] on notes where that seems easier for you. Purpose: to exercise higher tones on dark vowels.

[a    ɛ    i    ɔ    u          u    ɔ    i    ɛ    a]

**Additional reading**

*For proof that there are many paths to success, read the intriguing and often contradictory beliefs of opera stars in:*
*Great Singers on Great Singing* by Jerome Hines. Doubleday, Garden City, NY, 1982.

*Dozens of exercises for range extension are given in:*
*Coffin's Overtones of Bel Canto* by Berton Coffin. Scarecrow Press, Metuchen, NJ, 1980.

# 11 Understanding Your Vocal Instrument

*Physically, how does the voice work? How can I keep it healthy?*

## The voice as a musical instrument

All musical instruments have three essential elements:

- a *motor,* which provides and transmits energy;
- a *vibrator,* which converts the energy into audible vibrations (musical pitches); and
- a *resonator,* which strengthens the tones and modifies them by selectively strengthening certain overtones.

A part of the musician's body may provide one or two of the basic elements. A trumpet's motor, for instance, is the player's breath and the vibrator is the player's lips, while the brass tubing forms the resonator. What are the three basic elements in a violin? a clarinet? a bass drum? a piano?

The human voice has a fourth element, an articulator, which forms speech sounds. No other instrument can produce words. Even without the power of articulation, the voice transmits moods and emotions through a wide variety of tone colors. With articulation adding exact meaning and poetic appeal, the voice hás tremendous potential to communicate emotions.

All four elements of the voice must coordinate perfectly to produce the freest, most expressive singing. They are as follows:

1. *Motor,* or actuator: breath pressure, coming from the lungs.
2. *Vibrators:* vocal bands or cords, located in the larynx. Breath flow sets them in motion, and they produce a buzzing sound that is our basic vocal tone.
3. *Resonators:* the entire passageway from the vocal cords up to the lips and nose. The largest flexible, therefore alterable, resonators are the pharynx and mouth. Inflexible resonators include the nasal passages and, perhaps, the sinuses. Acoustical science has not yet answered all of our questions about resonance.
4. *Articulators:* the flexible tongue and lips acting against the inflexible teeth and hard palate, subject also to the angle of the jaw.

## What's behind your Adam's apple?

When all goes well, we sing without knowing or thinking anything about our throats. However, a time may come when we are sick or we feel other vocal problems, and then it is helpful to know the most important parts of the vocal instrument and how they work. You can easily learn about them with the help of Figure 11.1, referenced by numbers all through the following explanations.

Air from the lungs rises through the right and left bronchial tubes, which join to form the *trachea* (#1, windpipe). Just above your breastbone you can feel the bumpy partial rings of cartilage that hold the windpipe open. The only

**Figure 11.1**

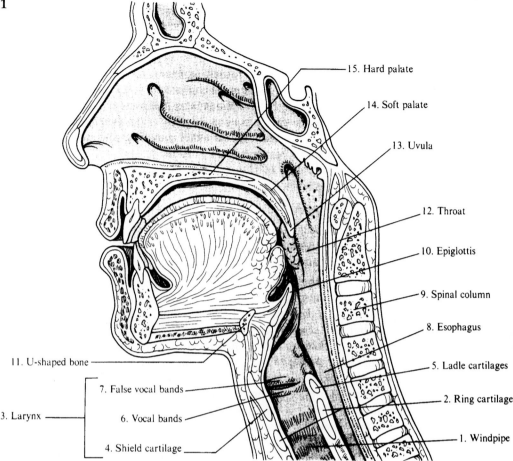

15. Hard palate

14. Soft palate

13. Uvula

12. Throat

10. Epiglottis

9. Spinal column

8. Esophagus

5. Ladle cartilages

2. Ring cartilage

1. Windpipe

11. U-shaped bone

7. False vocal bands

6. Vocal bands

4. Shield cartilage

3. Larynx

complete ring is the top one, the *cricoid cartilage* (#2, ring cartilage). It is larger than the rest and forms the base of the *larynx* (#3, voice box).

Practice saying the word "larynx" to rhyme with "rare inks"; its plural, "larynges," rhymes with "hinges."

If your larynx is large, it forms a bump called the "Adam's apple." If it is smaller, it may be more difficult to locate.

The part of the larynx that can be felt under the skin is the *thyroid cartilage* (#4, shield cartilage). It is named both for its shape, as seen from the front, and its vital function of protecting the top of the air passage from closing. Without it, we could be strangled by a tight collar or any other pressure on the neck. The shield cartilage has two sides that meet in front to form the Adam's apple.

The forward ends of the vocal folds are attached to the inside surface of the shield cartilage. They stretch over the top of the open windpipe, and at the rear end they are attached to two smaller cartilages, the right and left *arytenoid cartilages* (#5, ladle cartilages, located there but hidden in the tissue). The ladles slide along the upper surface of the ring cartilage. A complex system of muscles enables the arytenoids to move together and apart and to tip either forward and back or to the side, always moving counter to each other. The vocal folds are always close to each other at the front ends, but the arytenoids pull them apart at the rear when we breathe in and bring them together again when we speak or sing.

The ring, the shield, and the two ladles form the stiff framework of the larynx. Cartilages are flexible in children, harden as they mature, and eventually turn

**Figure 11.2**

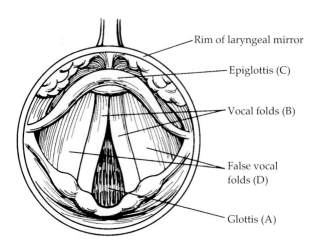

Rim of laryngeal mirror

Epiglottis (C)

Vocal folds (B)

False vocal
folds (D)

Glottis (A)

to bone. This is one of several reasons why voice quality changes with age. The inner surfaces of the larynx are covered with *mucous membrane*. When it is irritated by infection, you have "laryngitis" and may lose your voice.

What really interests us are the *vocal folds* (#6). Commonly called the vocal cords, they are called vocal bands or vocal folds in most recent scientific writing. The mass of the vocal bands consists of the thyro-arytenoid muscles (named for the cartilages where their ends are attached). Their edges, where the finest adjustments for singing take place, are formed of a white membrane that also covers their undersurfaces. When the bands are apart, the space between them is called the *glottis*, shown in Figure 11.2.

Just above the vocal folds are two similar bands, called the *false vocal folds* (#7). They play no role in voice production, but the space between the true and the false cords may be a significant resonator.

Directly behind the larynx is the top of the *esophagus* (#8, food pipe), which is closed flat against the *spinal column* (#9) except when something passes through it, going to the stomach.

Food and drink going to the esophagus have to cross over the larynx without falling into it. The top of the larynx is guarded by a leaf-shaped cartilage, the *epiglottis* (#10). Attached to the upper front edge of the shield cartilage, the epiglottis stands nearly upright most of the time, then falls down and back when we swallow, completely covering the larynx. When it fails to work properly, we choke.

The *hyoid bone* (#11, U-shaped bone) is located above the larynx at the base of the tongue; you may be able to feel the ends of it on either side of your neck just below the jaw. It forms part of the framework from which the larynx is suspended. You can sense this flexible suspension system if you use the backs of your fingers on either side of your larynx and move it from side to side.

The open space that forms our main resonator for singing is the *pharynx* (#12, throat). When you yawn in front of the mirror, you can see the moist back wall of the pharynx. If your pharynx is irritated by infection, you have pharyngitis, which is often painful but does not always involve losing your voice. The open space extends upward to form the naso-pharynx, which is closely connected to the nasal passages.

When you are looking in the mirror to find your pharynx, you can't help noticing your *uvula* (Latin for "little grape," #13), which hangs down from the *velum* (#14, soft palate). The soft palate can hang down and hide your pharynx, or it can rise up to expose quite a bit of the pharyngeal wall.

Raising and lowering the soft palate determines how much of your breath passes through your nose and how much through your mouth. If your soft palate is too low, too much breath passes through the nose and your tone sounds nasal. If your soft palate is too high, it can seal off the nasal passage so that you cannot say [m] or [n], and you sound like a person stopped up with a cold. Most voice teachers recommend keeping the palate high but not closing off the nasal passages.

In front of the soft palate is the bony *hard palate* (#15). By running your tongue back along the roof of your mouth you can feel where the hard palate ends.

Above the palate are the nasal passages, left and right. They are separated by a bony partition (septum). The sides of the nasal passages are lined with irregular projections that serve, like the surface of a radiator, to warm the air as it goes by.

Other parts of the vocal mechanism—the tongue, lips, jaw, and teeth—are all familiar and visible.

## Vocal health

As a basis for understanding vocal health, let's focus more closely on the vocal folds themselves. Figure 11.2 shows how they appear to a laryngologist looking down a person's throat with a dental mirror. The vocal folds are seen while closing to make a sound but are not yet fully closed.

At the center of the picture is a shaded space, the *glottis* (A), which opens into the windpipe. On either side of the glottis are the vocal folds (B). In this mirror image, the point where the vocal folds meet at the front of the larynx is toward the top of the picture but out of sight, hidden underneath the erect epiglottis (C). The rear end of the vocal folds is toward the bottom of the picture, also out of sight. The vocal bands look white and smooth when they are rested and healthy and pinkish after vigorous use. To either side of the white vocal bands, we see the pink upper surface of the false vocal folds (D), which hide all but the central part of the vocal folds from our view.

Here are some essential facts about the vocal bands:

1.  They are tiny. To visualize them, think that a soprano's vocal folds are stretched over a round opening with about the same diameter as a dime. A bass's are stretched over an opening the size of a nickel. We ask these small muscles to do remarkable feats for us.

2.  On most tones in your range, your vocal folds touch each other and separate again once for each vibration. For instance, if you sing middle C, which is in everyone's range, your vocal folds touch each other 262 times per second. They also part 262 times per second and let 262 puffs of air escape, initiating a wave movement in the air. A listener hears this wave as a tone with the pitch we call middle C and a frequency of 262 Hz (Hertz, or cycles per second).

When a man sings the C below middle C, his folds touch each other only 131 times per second, but if a woman sings the C above middle C, there are 524 such events. A soprano's high C has 1,048 vibrations, but at that speed the folds probably do not really touch each other. Can you imagine how many thousands of times the folds open and close in a song? Clearly, if there is anything rough, inefficient, or unnecessarily forceful about the singing tone, the contact edges of the vocal folds will be subjected to considerable friction, even chafing.

3.  Like the diaphragm, the vocal folds have no proprioceptive nerves, no way of telling us if they are being hurt. Nature wants to assure that the vocal folds always function and never shy away from pain. Any throat pain that we experience comes not from the vocal folds but from overworked muscles or infected tissues nearby.

4.  When our vocal folds are abused or infected, the body seeks to heal them by sending extra liquids to the scene: extra mucus to cover their surfaces and extra blood to heal internal damage. Increased blood supply turns the vocal folds pink or red, and they swell up.

5.  When the folds swell slightly, the first sign of trouble may be hoarseness, meaning that the edges are not closing perfectly and air is escaping between them. They may be unable to form the thin edges needed for high tones. If we go on trying to talk and sing, we may develop pain, as nearby muscles strain to take over the work of the vocal folds. If the vocal folds swell too much, their edges become bumpy, perhaps unable to meet and form tones at all. Then we lose our voices and have to rest them until the swelling goes down.

## Vocal overuse

The facts you have learned about the vocal folds explain why *overuse causes more voice problems than any other factor.* Enthusiastic, energetic singers love to socialize and enjoy expressing their emotions. It's not surprising that many of us overuse our voices.

What does "overuse" mean? The medical term is "hyperfunction," which includes the following:

- shouting, for instance, cheering at a sports event;
- loud talking and laughing, for instance, at a noisy party;
- insistent talking, as when we try to dominate others;
- talking or singing over the noise of a moving car or other machinery;
- coughing and throat clearing, which violently rub the bands against each other;
- singing at an inappropriate pitch level, as when one is placed in the wrong section of a choir; and
- singing longer and louder than we can do with comfort, whether that means singing with a rock band or getting carried away at an exciting choral rehearsal.

The limits of safe vocal use differ a great deal from one individual to another. Most of us learn our limits by the unhappy experience of hoarseness or temporary voice loss. Fortunately, our vocal folds are resilient; with enough rest, they usually repair themselves. We only need to be aware of trouble signs and stop doing whatever is causing the abuse.

I love to cheer at a football game, but if I can't sing for three or four days afterward, was the fun worth it?

## Damaged voices

You have learned how and why the vocal folds swell up to protect and heal themselves in cases of overuse. If overuse continues and the folds do not get enough rest to repair themselves, a persistent bump called a vocal node or nodule may develop on the edge of one or both folds. Nodes prevent the folds from closing correctly and cause reduction of range and volume. *Only a physician can correctly diagnose vocal nodes.*

If you experience persistent hoarseness, consult a physician to find out whether you have nodes and what treatment you need. In the early stages nodes are soft; they often heal with a few weeks of rest and reduced voice use. In later stages they grow progressively harder and require more rest to heal. Very seldom will a physician recommend surgical removal. (Never undertake surgery without a second or third medical opinion.)

If your folds develop nodes, don't necessarily blame your voice teacher, who sees you for only a short time each week and cannot possibly monitor all your activities. Your physician can recommend a speech therapist who will help you to identify vocally abusive habits in your daily life and replace them with healthful ones.

*Avoiding trouble*

Colds and influenzas are caused by a variety of viruses; we can be immunized against some of them but not all. Viruses are transmitted through the air when people cough and sneeze, but often they are introduced into our respiratory system by our own hands. When you shake hands with someone or hold the handle on the seat of a bus, you have no idea what viruses may be present. Wash your hands regularly and keep them away from your eyes, nose, lips, and mouth.

When you have been exposed to a virus, keep your first line of respiratory defense strong: *Keep your vocal tract moist.*

Your entire vocal tract is lined with mucous membrane, which produces moisture. We tend to notice mucus only when sickness has made it thick and annoying, but the constant, unnoticed production of mucus is essential to our health and comfort. Particles of foreign matter and microorganisms that land on mucous membrane stick to the wet surface and are carried away on the cleansing stream of moisture. If the membrane is dry, foreign particles are in irritating contact with body tissue and microorganisms have an opportunity to attack.

Heated and air-conditioned buildings, as well as automobiles and airplanes, usually have air that is unnaturally dry. Regular use of an ultrasonic vaporizer, especially in your sleeping room, may save you from many respiratory infections. It also helps to drink lots of liquids, especially water at medium temperature. Avoid diuretics, like coffee, which drain moisture from our tissues.

While keeping your humidity high, you can also keep your immunity as high as possible with reasonable rest, avoidance of stress, good nourishment that includes vitamin C, and, yes, a good mental attitude. Avoid letting your body become chilled because viruses thrive at a temperature somewhat lower than our normal body temperature. After long exposure to cold, a warm bath or shower may help raise your resistance.

Tobacco smoke obviously dries out our throat tissues. Marijuana smoke is even hotter because it is unfiltered. Don't smoke. Problems with cocaine and crack have been described by Dr. Van Lawrence in *The NATS Journal.*

If, in spite of all your care, you still catch a cold, drink liquids, rest, and reduce the amount you use your voice. Use caution with respect to medication. If you lose your voice, no magic potion will restore it. Remember that antihistamines, which stop your nose from running, also dry your throat.

Aspirin and products that contain aspirin dilate the capillaries that supply blood to the throat tissues so that the thin walls of the dilated capillaries can rupture and hemorrhage. Singers should use nonaspirin products for pain relief.

As for singing and voice lessons while you have a cold, follow your teacher's advice. If vocal rest is in order, that means

- talking quietly and less than usual;
- no singing, shouting, or laughing; and
- no whistling or loud whispering, both of which use the vocal cords.

For any vocal disorder that lasts more than three or four days, see a physician who will examine your vocal cords. Before your office visit, study again the vocal anatomy described in this chapter. As an informed patient, you can ask better questions and help the doctor to help you.

*Additional reading*    *The grandfather of voice books, now revised and in its second quarter century:*
*Keep Your Voice Healthy* (2d ed.) by Friedrich Brodnitz, M.D. College-Hill Press, 1987.

*The NATS Journal,* published by the National Association of Teachers of Singing, contains invaluable articles on vocal health and the latest research in vocal science. These journals can be found in your local public or college library. NATS also publishes a collection of past articles entitled *Vocal Health and Science* edited by Ingo Titze and Robert T. Sataloff, M.D.

# 12 A Vocabulary for Music

*Guiding questions:*

*Do I have a "musical ear"? What vocabulary is necessary to communicate with other musicians? What does "in a key" mean? What is a scale? How do musicians think about rhythm? What is a measure? What is syncopation? What can I learn from looking at a piece of printed music?*

YOU may not need this chapter if you already play an instrument and read notes. If you do need it, read it anytime on your own or whenever your teacher assigns it.

When I meet a new acquaintance and mention that I teach singing, that person often responds with excuses about a lack of musical background. Here are some things people say and answers I like to give if the other person wants to listen:

"Oh, I don't know a thing about music!" *Yes, you do. You are familiar with a tremendous amount of music. You just need a vocabulary to talk about it.*

"I hated piano lessons when I was a kid, but now I wish I'd kept on with them." *Don't feel guilty about your childhood music lessons. If music has a high enough priority for you, you can still learn.*

"I'd love to sing, but my family all say I have a tin ear." Sing anyway, and enjoy it. When you find the right group of people to sing with, you will fit right in.

You do not need to apologize because other people had music lessons or home experiences that you did not have. Whatever you learn, starting now, will enrich your life through increased awareness of the music all around you.

## What is a musical ear?

Musicians do not all have a mysterious faculty that others lack. Everyone has a "musical ear" to some degree. Like other mental skills, the ability to remember and reproduce musical pitches is highly individual; it varies a great deal from person to person, and it improves with training.

A few persons have so-called perfect pitch, the ability to name a pitch that is heard or to sing any note at will. Most professional musicians have some degree of "relative pitch," which is the ability to recognize or to sing particular notes with some reliability. Neither perfect nor relative pitch is essential for you to learn to sing melodies easily and correctly.

Are you "tone-deaf"? No; probably no physically normal person is tone-deaf. It is contradictory that people call themselves tone-deaf when they are perfectly able to hear the difference between two melodies and even to hear wrong notes or out of tune notes. People who believe that they are tone-deaf simply have not developed the ear-to-brain-to-throat coordination that singing requires.

Occasionally, a "pitch problem" disappears as soon as the singer realizes what vocal register to use; other cases require more time and experience in a supportive group-singing environment.

## Pitch

When Maria in *The Sound of Music* started to teach music to the von Trapp children, she made up a song, "Do-Re-Mi" (page 34). The seven syllables *Do, Re, Mi, Fa, So, La, Ti,* are widely used names for the notes that we call C, D, E, F, G, A, B. Because we hear tones as being "higher" and "lower," it makes sense to arrange the names of the tones vertically, like this:

| | | |
|---|---|---|
| 8 | C | Do |
| 7 | B | Ti |
| 6 | A | La |
| 5 | G | So |
| 4 | F | Fa |
| 3 | E | Mi |
| 2 | D | Re |
| 1 | C | Do |

Sing up a scale, starting from the lowest note and singing "One, two, three . . ." (Whether or not you start on C is not important right now.) Sing back down the scale: "Eight, seven, six . . ." (It sounds like the Christmas song "Joy to the World.") Sing up and down the scale again, singing letter names: "C, D, E . . ." Sing up and down a third time, singing the names of the syllables: "Do, Re, Mi . . ." Now you will see the connections between Maria's song and the notes that we call a *C major scale*.

The C major scale is written like this, using alternate lines and spaces of a musical staff.

    C   D   E   F   G   A   B   C   B   A   G   F   E   D   C

If you have a keyboard, you can easily play this scale. The black keys are in groups of two and three; any white key that is immediately to the left of a group of two black keys is a C. Start there and play the white keys in order from left to right until you reach the next C; you will hear an ascending scale. Play them again from right to left; you will hear a descending scale.

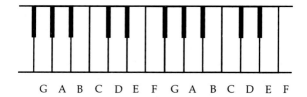

    G  A  B  C  D  E  F  G  A  B  C  D  E  F

The distance between two neighboring notes is called a scale step, but not all steps are equal. Between some pairs of white keys there is a black key, but there is none between others because they already sound as close to each other as notes can sound in our musical system. The smallest distance between notes is called a half-step; it is the distance between adjacent keys, whether white or black. Most scale steps are a whole-step apart, which is the distance between two keys that have another one, white or black, between them.

*Do* is at both the bottom and the top of our scale because the series repeats itself both upward and downward, as high and as low as your ear can hear. Below *Do* there is always another *Ti;* above *Do* there is always another *Re.*

What is the relationship between the lower *Do* and the higher one? They are different notes, but they sound so much alike that they have the same name.

Why? The vibrations of the upper *Do* are exactly twice as fast as those of the lower one. If you play them together, every second vibration of the upper *Do* will coincide with a vibration of the lower *Do*. (You don't hear separate vibrations because they are much too fast. See the frequencies of various C's on page 69.)

The distance between the two *Do's* is an *octave* (from Latin *octo*, eight). In a voice class it is important to realize that women and men usually sing an octave apart. If women sing *in unison*, they all sing the same notes at the same time. If we say that a mixed group of people sing in unison, we are overlooking the fact that women and men are actually singing an octave apart. When men sing the songs in this book, they sound an octave lower than the notes are written. (Tenors in choir also sing an octave lower than their music is written.) If your teacher is of the opposite sex from you, you may need some practice before you can recognize and sing back the pitches that she or he sings for you.

Sometimes singers avoid the extremes of their range by changing a song, singing a few notes or a phrase an octave higher or an octave lower than written. At other times singers change notes just to use the extremes of their range, especially to make the ending of a song more exciting by singing it high.

Whole-steps and half-steps are also known as seconds, and the other *intervals* (distances between notes) have simple numerical names: a third, a fourth, and so on. Each interval has its distinctive sound, and with practice you can learn to recognize them, but it is not necessary right now. For the present, you may learn your songs "by rote," that is, by hearing them repeatedly.

# Keys

Sometimes a student asks, "What key is good for my voice?" First, we have to talk about what "in a key" means and the difference between the concepts of key and range.

Most pieces of music reach a point of finality at the end. If the piece were interrupted, you would be dissatisfied. Test this by asking someone to play "Michael, Row the Boat Ashore" on the piano and stop without playing the last note. There is a sense of incompleteness, even frustration.

To say that "Michael, Row the Boat Ashore" is in the key of C means that we need to hear the note C and the chord of C at the end in order to have a feeling of completeness. The fact that we are hearing tones of a certain scale leads us to expect a certain note at the end. A trained musician would say in this case that hearing tones of the C Major scale leads us to expect that the song will end with the tonic note of C and the tonic chord of C Major.

We grasp this system intuitively because we have heard thousands of pieces of music written in what is called the *tonal system*.

Test this concept again by having "Michael, Row the Boat Ashore" played with a "wrong" chord at the end!

Quite different from this is the concept of range, the distance between the lowest and highest notes of a song. Most people are comfortable singing "Michael, Row the Boat Ashore" in the key of C. If is too low for you, you might rather sing it in E Major or F Major. Changing the key of a piece is called transposing it, and singers often transpose song either up or down.

The tonic note of a song is not necessarily the lowest or the highest note of the song. And songs that are in your comfortable range are not necessarily all in the same key.

This is why the student's question mentioned earlier could not be answered easily. Two songs may be in the same key and yet have different ranges. What the student really wants to know is "Will the range of this song fit my voice?"

# Scales

The C Major scale is a useful model because its notes correspond to the lines and spaces of the musical staff without any added symbols. Also, the C Major scale can be played on the white keys of the keyboard. But the notes of C Major are not the only ones in our musical system. Other notes are used to enable us to sing in a variety of keys.

When we played the C Major scale we noticed that there were half-steps between notes 3 and 4 and notes 7 and 8. All other major scales have that same pattern. It is by hearing this pattern, even if you are unaware of it, that you recognize the tonic of a major key.

Here is an example: When we begin a scale on F, the third and fourth notes need to be a half-step apart. Since the third note is A, the fourth note must be B-flat, the note that is a half-step higher than A. Musical notation shows this by placing a symbol called a flat at the beginning of the piece; the flat changes every written B in the piece to a B-flat. An F scale looks like this:

F    G    A    B♭    C    D    E    F    E    D    C    B♭    A    G    F

Just as a flat sign lowers a note by a half-step, a sharp sign raises a note by a half-step. Some notes have more than one name. Each of the black keys on a keyboard has two names, a sharp name and a flat name. A-sharp (a half-step higher than A) is written differently from B-flat (a half-step lower than B) on the musical staff but sounds exactly the same and is the same key on the piano.

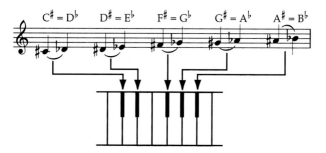

If A-sharp (A♯) and B-flat (B♭) sound exactly the same when played on the piano, why do they have different names? Because they are used in the context of different scales, which will be confusing to read if they are not written systematically.

The seven tones of C Major plus the five tones that are played by black keys make a total of twelve tones in every octave. Played in order, the twelve tones form the *chromatic scale*. Any of the twelve can serve as the tonic of a key. This *tonal system* is typical of *Western music*, defined as the dominant artistic music of Western Europe and the Western Hemisphere. Other cultures—for instance, those of China and India—have evolved other musical systems of music with their own special features.

The great strength of Western music is the flexibility of tonal music. We can even change key ("modulate") in the middle of a song, meaning that the ear can be fooled into accepting a new note as a temporary tonic. This is achieved by the use of temporary alterations of the scale, called "chromatics." When you see flats or sharps in a piece of music, something like this may be going on. If you take a course in harmony, you will learn more about this.

So far we have not mentioned *minor keys*, but they have great charm and are not always sad, as people often think. To hear a minor scale, go back to the keyboard and play a scale on white keys from A to A. This is called the natural minor scale of A Minor, and its most important feature is the half-step between notes 2 and 3 (rather than 3 and 4 as in a major scale). Notes 6 and 7 are flexible in minor scales, often being raised a half-step at the composer's wish.

## Rhythm

Musical rhythm is also a flexible system and is primarily concerned with patterns of accents rather than with real time.

Babies notice repeated movements and sounds and respond to them with pleasure. The most primitive rhythm is simple repetition of a steady beat:

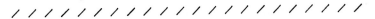

A baby notices such regularity and enjoys it, but does not respond the same way if strong beats are put in randomly, like this:

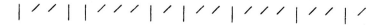

Pleasurable musical rhythm begins when the stronger beats occur in a pattern, like this four-beat pattern:

or this three-beat pattern:

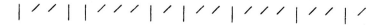

Most of the music we hear every day is organized in patterns of two, three, or four beats. In written music, the beginning of a beat pattern is shown by a vertical line called a *measure bar* or *bar line*. The music between two bar lines is one *measure*, or one *bar*, of music.

The note just to the right of the bar line is always a strong beat. It is called a *downbeat* because of the downward movement of a conductor's arm to start a measure. Often a phrase of music begins with an *upbeat*, which consists of one or two or more notes that prepare for the downbeat. Think of the melody to "He's Got the Whole World in His Hands." What word comes on the first downbeat? How many upbeat notes are there? What word comes on the second downbeat?

The diagrams of four- and three-beat patterns imply that downbeats are naturally louder than the beats in between, but that is not always so. When gospel singers clap, they usually clap after the downbeat, not with it. This creates strong accents that are perceived as offbeat rather than on the downbeat. Downbeats are established by means other than loudness, such as

- patterns of notes in the accompaniment that repeat once or twice in every measure,
- chord changes on the first beat of each measure, and
- word accents.

In addition to notes on the basic beats, there are notes that last more than one beat and other notes that occur faster than the basic beats. You have already noticed that notes all have oval heads. The longest note, called a whole note (normally four beats), is simply an empty oval. Adding a vertical stem makes a half-note (two beats), filling it in makes a quarter note (one beat), and each added flag cuts the length of the note in half again.

Ways to produce other note lengths include combining consecutive notes of the same pitch with a curved line called a "tie," adding one-half to the length of a note with a dot, or bracketing three notes together with an indication that they take up the time value of two.

There can be a sense of surprise or fun when an event in the music suddenly goes against the pattern. Perhaps a strong high note comes on a beat that is normally weak and then holds over to the next strong beat. Perhaps an emphatic word occurs in a weak part of the measure; or perhaps when we expect a downbeat there is a rest instead, and the expected note comes a half-beat late. Such ways of shifting the measure accent are called *syncopation.*

## Looking at music

Even if you think you "can't read music," you can learn a lot by taking a close look at a song you want to learn in order to see what the printed page can tell you. As an example, let's use Schubert's "An die Musik" (To Music; page 160).

Just below the title of the song, in German and in English, is a small musical staff that shows the range of the song. Slightly lower down are two names, on the left the poet who wrote the words and on the right the composer of the music.

On the page are three *systems*, each made up of three lines of music, connected to each other by vertical lines at the left. Each line of music is written on a *staff* of five parallel lines. In each group of staves, the upper one contains the voice part with words below. The lower two staves, which are connected by all of the measure bars, are for the piano music. Most of the time the pianist's right hand plays from the upper staff and the left hand from the lower one, but crossovers also occur.

At the left of the upper two staves are fancy symbols called *G clefs,* which curl around the second line from the bottom; notes on this line are G's. The lowest staff has an *F clef,* formed of a curlicue and two dots to draw attention to the fourth line; notes on this line are F's. The midpoint between the upper and lower staves is *middle C,* which is written either on a partial line below the upper staff or on a partial line above the lower staff.

Immediately after the clefs there may be flat or sharp signs called the *key signature;* as explained previously, they determine what key the music is in. The key signature is repeated on every line.

Next comes a *meter signature,* or *time signature,* in this case a C with a vertical slash through it. This means that there are two beats per measure, each a half-note. A similar symbol, C without a slash, means four beats per measure, each a quarter-note. Other meter signatures consist of two numbers: The upper number tells how many beats are in a measure, and the lower one tells what kind of note stands for a beat.

"An die Musik" begins with a piano *introduction,* so the voice part has rest signs in the first two measures. At the end of measure 2 is a double bar line with two dots to its right; later you will come back to this point and sing the music over again, using the words of the second stanza.

There is another rest on the downbeat of measure 3, meaning that you sing just afterward. You have had a chance to hear how quickly the chords move in the piano part, and you can time your notes to match them. Look at your first note, and notice that in measure 2 the piano played that note four times; this will help you find your pitch in the next measure.

Looking ahead at your part, there are other rests where you can take a breath. You can take more breaths at punctuation marks or at other spots where the meaning of the words will not be disturbed. Many songs have no written rests at all; the composer assumes that you will find satisfactory places to breathe.

After the first stanza the piano plays an *interlude;* at the repeat bar (with dots to the left) the pianist goes back to measure 3. After the second stanza the pianist plays the interlude again, but now it is called a *postlude,* and it ends with the measure after the repeat bars.

Some folk and pop songs in this book have symbols above the vocal line to tell a pianist or guitarist what chords to play. The player decides how to play the chords, and it is not considered important for the notes to be exactly the same for every performance. In classical music, chord symbols are not used because the composer has written the notes of the accompaniment with care, expecting them always to be the same.

This introduction to musical scores may have raised more questions in your mind than it answered. At least, you can see that the score is a kind of roadmap, a chart from which you can get useful information even if you do not play an instrument. If this chapter has awakened your curiosity, you would enjoy learning more in a course on rudiments of music or a beginning piano class.

*Additional reading*

*For a clear, readable, thoroughly practical explanation of music symbols, based on tunes you already know:*
*Learn to Read Music* by Howard Shanet. Simon and Schuster, 1956.

# Songs

# America the Beautiful

Katherine Lee Bates

Samuel A. Ward

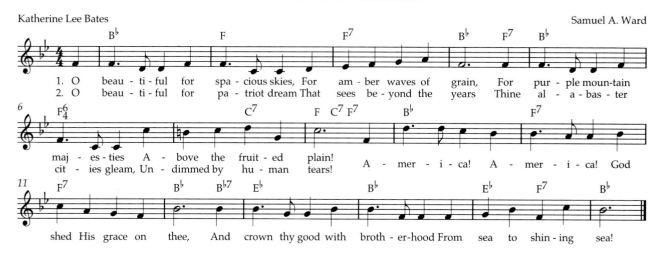

1. O beau-ti-ful for spa-cious skies, For am-ber waves of grain, For pur-ple moun-tain
2. O beau-ti-ful for pa-triot dream That sees be-yond the years Thine al-a-bas-ter

maj-es-ties A-bove the fruit-ed plain! A-mer-i-ca! A-mer-i-ca! God
cit-ies gleam, Un-dimmed by hu-man tears!

shed His grace on thee, And crown thy good with broth-er-hood From sea to shin-ing sea!

# De colores

Traditional

Mexico

De co-lo-res, _____ de co-lo-res se vis-ten los

cam-pos en la pri-ma-ve-ra; _____ De co-lo-res, _____

_____ de co-lo-res son los pa-ja-ri-llos que vie-nen de

fue-ra. _____ De co-lo-res, _____ de co-lo-res es

el ar-co-i-ris que ve-mos lu-cir, _____ y por

e-so los gran-des a-mo-res de mu-chos co-

lo-res me gus-tan a mi. _____ Y por mi.

*Literal translation: With colors the fields are dressed in the springtime, and also the birds that come from afar, the rainbow that shines above. That's why I have a great love for bright colors.*

Notes about these songs are on pages 261 and 278.

# Do-Re-Mi

Oscar Hammerstein II

Richard Rodgers

Doe, a deer, a fe - male deer, Ray, a drop of gol - den sun, _____

Me, a name I call my - self, Far, a long, long way to run, _____

Sew, a nee - dle pull - ing thread, _____ La, a note to fol - low sew, _____

Tea, a drink with jam and bread _____ that will bring us back to

do - oh - oh - oh! do! _____ Do - re - mi - fa - so - la - ti - do! _____

# Down in the Valley

Appalachia, U. S. A.

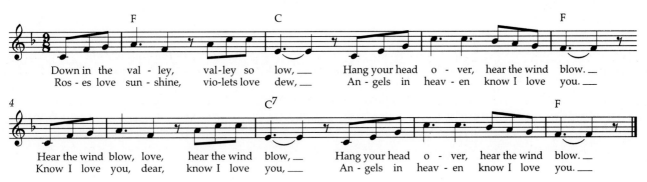

Down in the val - ley, val - ley so low, ___ Hang your head o - ver, hear the wind blow. __
Ros - es love sun - shine, vio - lets love dew, ___ An - gels in heav - en know I love you. __

Hear the wind blow, love, hear the wind blow, ___ Hang your head o - ver, hear the wind blow. __
Know I love you, dear, know I love you, ___ An - gels in heav - en know I love you. __

Notes about these songs are on page 261.

# He's Got the Whole World in His Hands

Traditional

Spiritual

1. He's got the whole _____ world _ in His hands, _ He's got the
2. He's got the wind and the rain ___ in His hands, _ He's got the
3. He's got the gamb - lin' ____ man ___ in His hands, _ He's got the

big, round ___ world _ in His hands, _ He's got the wide _____ world _
moon and the stars ___ in His hands, _ He's got the wind and the rain ___
ly - in' _____ man ___ in His hands, _ He's got the crap - shoot - in' man ___

*(all stanzas)*

in His hands, __ He's got the whole world in His hands.

4. He's got the little-bitsy baby in His hands . . . (sing three times)

5. He's got you and me, brother, in His hands,
   He's got you and me, sister, in His hands,
   He's got you and me, brother, in His hands . . .

6. Oh, He's got everybody in His hands . . . (sing three times)

Notes about this song are on page 261.

84

# Let There Be Peace on Earth

S. Miller and J. Jackson

Sy Miller and Jill Jackson

Notes about this song are on page 261.

# Michael, Row the Boat Ashore

Traditional

Spiritual

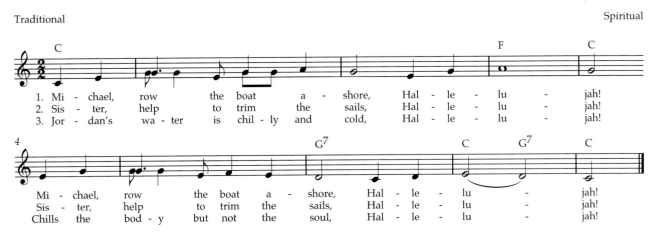

1. Mi - chael, row the boat a - shore, Hal - le - lu - jah!
2. Sis - ter, help to trim the sails, Hal - le - lu - jah!
3. Jor - dan's wa - ter is chil - ly and cold, Hal - le - lu - jah!

Mi - chael, row the boat a - shore, Hal - le - lu - jah!
Sis - ter, help to trim the sails, Hal - le - lu - jah!
Chills the bod - y but not the soul, Hal - le - lu - jah!

# Scarborough Fair

Traditional

England

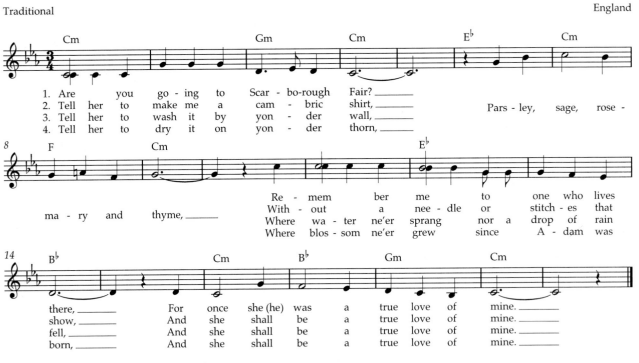

1. Are you go - ing to Scar - bo - rough Fair? _____
2. Tell her to make me a cam - bric shirt, _____
3. Tell her to wash it by yon - der wall, _____
4. Tell her to dry it on yon - der thorn, _____

Pars - ley, sage, rose -

ma - ry and thyme, _____

Re - mem - ber me to one who lives
With - out a nee - dle or stitch - es that
Where wa - ter ne'er sprang nor a drop of rain
Where blos - som ne'er grew since A - dam was

there, _____ For once she (he) was a true love of mine. _____
show, _____ And she shall be a true love of mine. _____
fell, _____ And she shall be a true love of mine. _____
born, _____ And she shall be a true love of mine. _____

Text when sung by a woman:

2. Tell him to bring me an acre of land, Parsley . . .
   Betwixt the wild ocean and yonder sea sand, And he . . .

3. Tell him to plough it with one ram's horn, Parsley . . .
   And sow it all over with one peppercorn, And he . . .

4. Tell him to reap it with a sickle of leather, Parsley . . .
   And bind it together with one peacock feather, And he . . .

Notes about these songs are on page 261.

# Shalom Chaverim

Traditional Israel

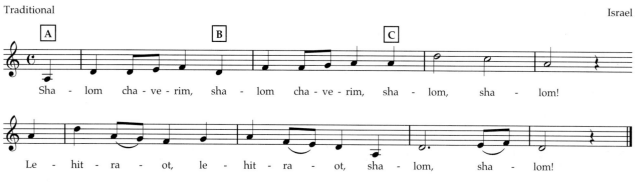

Sha - lom cha - ve - rim, sha - lom cha - ve - rim, sha - lom, sha - lom!

Le - hit - ra - ot, le - hit - ra - ot, sha - lom, sha - lom!

*Peace, friends, till we meet again.*

# She'll Be Comin' Round the Mountain

Southern United States

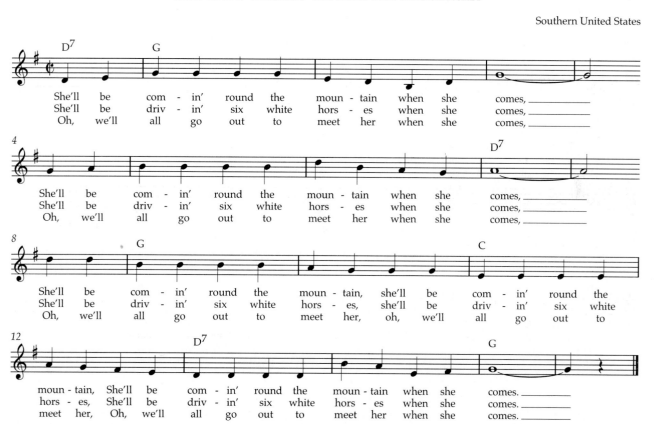

She'll be com - in' round the moun - tain when she comes, _____
She'll be driv - in' six white hors - es when she comes, _____
Oh, we'll all go out to meet her when she comes, _____

She'll be com - in' round the moun - tain when she comes, _____
She'll be driv - in' six white hors - es when she comes, _____
Oh, we'll all go out to meet her when she comes, _____

She'll be com - in' round the moun - tain, she'll be com - in' round the
She'll be driv - in' six white hors - es, she'll be driv - in' six white
Oh, we'll all go out to meet her, oh, we'll all go out to

moun - tain, She'll be com - in' round the moun - tain when she comes. _____
hors - es, She'll be driv - in' six white hors - es when she comes. _____
meet her, Oh, we'll all go out to meet her when she comes. _____

Notes about these songs are on pages 262 and 283.

# The Star-Spangled Banner

Francis Scott Key

John Stafford Smith

Notes about this song are on page 262.

# Viva la musica!

Michael Praetorius

Vi - va, vi - va la mu - si - ca! Vi - va, vi - va la mu - si - ca! Vi - va la mu - si - ca! Vi - va!

*Long live music!*

# When the Saints Go Marchin' In

Unknown

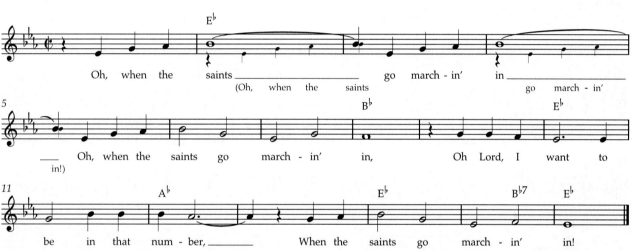

Oh, when the saints _____ go march - in' in _____
(Oh, when the saints go march - in'

_____ Oh, when the saints go march - in' in, Oh Lord, I want to
in!)

be in that num - ber, _____ When the saints go march - in' in!

Notes about these songs are on page 262.

# Auprès de ma blonde

Traditional

Normandie, France
*Arranged by J. G. P.*

1. Au jar - din de mon pè - re Les
2. La caill', la tour - te - rel - le Et
3. Ell' chan - te pour les fil - les Qui

lau - riers sont fleu - ris; _____ Au jar - din de mon pè - re Les
la jo - li per - drix, _____ La caill', la tour - te - rel - le, Et
n'ont point de ma - ri; _____ Ell' chan - te pour les fil - les Qui

lau - riers sont fleu - ris; _____ Tous les oi - seaux du mon - de Vont
la jo - li per - drix _____ Et la blan - che co - lom - be Qui
n'ont point de ma - ri; _____ C'est pas pour moi qu'ell' chan - te, Car

*Literal translation: (1) In my father's garden/ the laurels are blooming;/ birds from everywhere/ go there to nest . . . /*
*(2) The quail, the turtledove,/ the pretty partridge,/ and the white dove,/ which sings day and night . . . /*
*(3) The dove sings for the girls/ who have no husbands,/ but it does not sing for me,/ because I have a handsome one/*

Notes about this song are on pages 262 and 280.

*(Refrain) Beside my blonde wife,/ how good it is to sleep!*

# Cielito lindo

Traditional

Mexico
*Arranged by J. G. P.*

*Literal translation: (1) From the high mountains a pair of dark eyes came down to me, beautiful Heaven! precious eyes!*
*(2) The bird that leaves its first nest and then goes back does not find its lost love again.*
*(3) That beauty mark that you have near your mouth, don't give it to anyone; it belongs to me.*

Notes about this song are on pages 262 and 278.

# Cielito lindo

Traditional

Mexico
*Arranged by J. G. P.*

1. De la Sie - rra Mo - re - na vie - nen ba - jan - do, vie -
2. Pa - ja - ro ____ que a-ban - do - na su ____ pri - mer ni - do, su __
3. E - se lu - nar que tie - nes, cie - li - to lin - do, jun -

- nen ba - jan - do, _____ Un par de o - ji - tos
____ pri - mer ni - do, _____ Re - gre - sa ____ y ya no en -
- to a la bo - ca, _____ No se lo ____ des a

ne - gros, cie - li - to lin - do, de ____ con - tra - ban - do. _____
cuen - tra, cie - li - to lin - do, el ____ bien per - di - do. _____
na - die, cie - li - to lin - do, que a __ mi me to - ca. _____

*Literal translation: (1) From the high mountains a pair of dark eyes came down to me, beautiful Heaven! precious eyes!*
*(2) The bird that leaves its first nest and then goes back does not find its lost love again.*
*(3) That beauty mark that you have near your mouth, don't give it to anyone; it belongs to me.*

Notes about this song are on pages 262 and 278.

Ay, ay, ay, ay, _____ can - ta y no llo - res, _____ Por -
que can - tan - do se_a - le - gran, cie - li - to lin - do, los _
___ co - ra - zo - nes. _____ zo - nes. _____

1., 3., 5.
to Refrain

2., 4., 6.
to Verses
Final

# Cockles and Mussels

Traditional

Ireland, ca. 1750
*Arranged by V. A. C., revised by J. G. P.*

Notes about this song are on page 262.

wheeled her wheel - bar - row through
each wheeled their bar - row through } streets broad and nar - row, Cry - ing

"Cock - les ___ and mus - sels, __ a - live, a - live, oh!"

**Slower, sadly**
*p*

3. But she died of a fe - ver, And none could re - lieve her, And

*with pedal*

that was the end of poor Mol - ly Ma - lone, But her

# Cockles and Mussels

Traditional

Ireland, ca. 1750
*Arranged by V. A. C., revised by J. G. P.*

Notes about this song are on page 262.

wheeled her wheel - bar - row through
each wheeled their bar - row through
streets broad and nar - row, Cry - ing

"Cock - les ___ and mus - sels, __ a - live, a - live, oh!"

**Slower, sadly**

3. But she died of a fe - ver, And none could re - lieve her, And

*with pedal*

that was the end of poor Mol - ly Ma - lone, But her

ghost wheels her bar-row Through streets broad and nar-row, Cry-ing

"Cock-les __ and mus-sels, _ a - live, a - live, oh!"

A - live a - live, oh! __ A - live, a - live, oh!" _ Cry-ing

"Cock-les __ and mus-sels, _ a - live, a - live, oh!" _____

# Early One Morning

Traditional

England
*Arranged by V. A. C. and J. G. P.*

1. Ear - ly one morn - ing, just as the sun was
3. Re - mem - ber the vows that you made to your

ris - ing, I heard a maid sing in the val - ley be - low:
Ma - ry, Re - mem - ber the bow'r where you vowed to be true!

"Oh, don't de - ceive me! Oh, nev - er leave me! How could you

Notes about this song are on page 262.

# Early One Morning

Traditional

England
*Arranged by V. A. C. and J. G. P.*

1. Ear - ly one morn - ing, just as the sun was
3. Re-mem-ber the vows _ that you made _ to your

ris - ing, I heard a maid _ sing _ in the val - ley be - low:
Ma - ry, Re - mem - ber the bow'r _ where you vowed _ to be true!

"Oh, don't de - ceive _ me! Oh, nev - er leave _ me! How _ could you

Notes about this song are on page 262.

use _ a _ poor _ maid-en so?" 2. "Oh, gay is the gar - land, _

4. Thus sang the poor maid - en, her

fresh _ are the ros - es I culled from the gar - den to

sor - row be - wail - ing, Thus sang the poor maid _ in the

bind _ on your brow.

val - ley be - low:

Oh, don't de - ceive _ me! Oh, nev - er

leave _ me! How _ could you use _ a _ poor _ maid-en so?"

# High Barbaree

Traditional

Sea Chantey
*Arranged by V. A. C. and J. G. P.*

Notes about this song are on page 262.

on the coast of High Bar - ba - ree.  4. But oh, it was a

sad sight, and griev-ed us full sore, __ Blow high, __ blow low, __ And

so __ sail-ed we, __ To see them all a - drown-ing as __ they tried to swim a -

shore, __ A - sail-ing down all on the coast of High __ Bar - ba - ree.

# I Know Where I'm Goin'

Traditional

County Antrim, Ireland
*Arranged by Herbert Hughes*

Notes about this song are on page 263.

leath-er,      Combs to buc-kle my  hair,      And a  ring for ev-'ry  fin-ger.

Some    say he's bad,      But  I   say he's

bon - ny,    The  fair - est  of  them  all,     My ___ hand-some, win-some

John-ny.                              Feath-er-beds are  soft,      And

# Love Will Find Out the Way

Traditional

England

*Arranged by J. G. P.*

Over the ___ moun - tains And ___ o - ver the
Where there is ___ no place For the glow - worm to

waves, Un - der the ___ foun - tains And ___
lie, Where there is ___ no space For re -

un - der the graves, Un - der floods _____ that are
ceipt of a fly, Where the midge _____ does not

Notes about this song are on page 263.

And some do sup-pose him, poor __ thing, to be blind. But if ne'er so close you wall him, Do the best that you __ may, Blind __ love, if so you call __ him, Will __ find out his way.

*rit.*

# El Tecolote

Traditional

Mexico
*Arranged by J. G. P.*

Te-co-lo-te de Gua-dia-na, pa-ja-ro ma-dru-ga-dor, Te-co-lo-te de Gua-dia-na, Pa-ja-ro ma-dru-ga-dor, Pa-ra que vue-las de no-che, pa-ra que vue-las de

*Literal translation: Guadiana owl,/ morning bird, why do you fly at night,/*

Notes about this song are on pages 263 and 279.

*keeping the daytime for yourself?/ Poor owl,/ you are already tired of flying.*

# The Turtle Dove

English Folk Song
*Arranged by V. A. C.*

**pp** 1. Fare thee well, my dear, I must be __ gone, And __ leave you __ for a -
**mp** 2. So __ fair thou art, my bon - ny __ lass, So __ deep in __ love am __
**mf** 3. The __ crow that's black, my lit - tle tur - tle dove, Shall __ change its __ col - ors __

while; For __ though __ I ___ go I'll __ come back a - gain, Though I
I; But I nev - er will prove false to the bon - ny lass I love, Till the
white Be - fore ___ I am false to the one __ that I love, The __

Notes about this song are on page 263.

116

roam ten thou-sand miles, my dear, Though I roam ten thou-sand miles.
stars fall from the sky, my dear, Till the stars fall from the sky.
noon-day shall be night, my dear, The __ noon-day shall be

night. O __ yon-der doth sit that lit-tle tur-tle dove, He doth sit on __ yon-der high

tree, A - mak-ing a moan for the loss of his love, As __ I will do for

thee, my dear, As __ I will do for thee. _____

# Walk Together, Children

Traditional

Spiritual

*Arranged by V. A. C. and J. G. P.*

Notes about this song are on page 263.

Prom-ised Land. Goin' to (mourn) and nev-er ti - ah, _____
(Going) (shout) (tire)

(mourn) and nev-er ti - ah, (mourn) and nev-er
(shout) (shout)

Ending

ti - ah, Great camp-meet-ing in the Prom-ised Land!

Alternate ending

Great camp-meet-ing in that Prom-ised Land!

*mf*

*cresc. e rit.*

*mf*

*f*

*f*

# It Was a Lover and His Lass

William Shakespeare

Thomas Morley
*Arranged by J. G. P.*

1. It was a lov - er and his lass, With a
2. This car - ol they be - gan that hour, With a

hay, and a ho, and a hay      no - ni - no, and a hay _____
hay, and a ho, and a hay      no - ni - no, and a hay _____

__ no - ni - no - ni     no.      That
__ no - ni - no - ni     no.      How

Notes about this song are on page 263.

# It Was a Lover and His Lass

William Shakespeare

Thomas Morley
*Arranged by J. G. P.*

1. It was a lov - er and his lass, With a
2. This car - ol they be - gan that hour, With a

hay, and a ho, and a hay no - ni - no, and a hay _____
hay, and a ho, and a hay no - ni - no, and a hay _____

_ no - ni - no - ni no.        That
_ no - ni - no - ni no.        How

Notes about this song are on page 263.

# When Laura Smiles

Philip Rosseter

Philip Rosseter
*Edited by J. G. P.*

Notes about this song are on page 264.

And her speech with ev - er - flow - ing mu - sic doth re -
For she with her di - vine beau - ties all the world sub -

pair The cru - el wounds of sor - row and un - tamed de - spair.
dues And fills with heav'n - ly spir - its my _____ hum - ble muse.

# Since First I Saw Your Face

Thomas Ford

Thomas Ford
*Realization by J. G. P.*

Since first I saw your face I re-solved To hon - or and re-
If I ad-mire or praise you too much, That fault you may for -

nown _____ you. If now I be dis - dained, I _____ wish my
give _____ me. Or if my hands had strayed but a touch, Then

heart had nev - er known _____ you. What, I that loved and
just - ly might you leave _____ me. I asked you leave, you

Notes about this song are on page 264.

128

you      that liked, Shall   we   be - gin to   wran - gle?      No,   no,
bade    me love,  Is    now    the time to    chide   me?        No,   no,

no,    my heart   is   fast, And can   -  not dis - en - tan  -  gle.
no,    I'll   love    you   still What for  -  tune e'er   be - tide   me.

# Since First I Saw Your Face

Thomas Ford

Thomas Ford
*Realization by J. G. P.*

Since first I saw your face I re-solved To hon - or and re-
If I ad - mire or praise you too much, That fault you may for-

nown _____ you. If now I be dis - dained, I _____ wish my
give _____ me. Or if my hands had strayed but a touch, Then

heart had nev - er known _____ you. What, I that loved and
just - ly might you leave _____ me. I asked you leave, you

Notes about this song are on page 264.

you that liked, Shall we be - gin to wran - gle? No, no,
bade me love, Is now the time to chide me? No, no,

no, my heart is fast, And can - not dis - en - tan - gle.
no, I'll love you still What for - tune e'er be - tide me.

# Man Is for the Woman Made

Peter Anthony Motteux

Henry Purcell
*Edited by V. A. C. and J. G. P.*

Notes about this song are on page 265.

# Man Is for the Woman Made

*(Low Key)*

Peter Anthony Motteux

Henry Purcell
*Edited by V. A. C. and J. G. P.*

Man, man, man is for ___ the ___ wom - an ___ made, And the wom - an made ___ for man. As the
(As the)
(Be she)

spur is for the jade, As the scab - bard for the
scep - ter's to be swayed, As for nights the ser - e -
wid - ow, be she maid, Be she wan - ton, be she

Notes about this song are on page 265.

135

# Dolce scherza

Poet unknown

Giacomo Antonio Perti
*Realization by J. G. P.*

Dol - ce _____ scher - za _ e dol - ce _____ ri - de va - go _____

lab - bro _ e spi - ra a - mor. Dol - ce _____ scher - za _ e

dol - ce _____ ri - de va - go _____ lab - bro _ e

*Literal translation: A lovely mouth sweetly teases and sweetly smiles, breathing love.*

Notes about this song are on pages 265 and 275.

*But it pleases you and then kills you; that's what it did to my heart.*

# Dolce scherza

Poet unknown

Giacomo Antonio Perti

*Realization by J. G. P.*

*Literal translation: A lovely mouth sweetly teases and sweetly smiles, breathing love.*

Notes about this song are on pages 265 and 275.

*But it pleases you and then kills you; that's what it did to my heart.*

# Vado ben spesso

Anonymous

Giovanni Bononcini
*Edited by J. G. P.*

Va - do ben spes-so can-gian-do __ lo - co,

Va - do ben spes - so can-gian-do __ lo - co, Ma non sò mai can-giar de-

si - o.

*Literal translation: I go often from place to place,/ but I never change my desire./*

Notes about this song are on pages 265 and 275.

*Always the same will be my love,/ and I shall be the same, too.*

# Vado ben spesso

Anonymous

Giovanni Bononcini
*Edited by J. G. P.*

*Literal translation: I go often from place to place,/ but I never change my desire./*

Notes about this song are on pages 265 and 275.

Va-do ben spes-so can-gian-do lo - co, Ma non sò mai,

ma non sò mai, ma _____ non sò mai can-giar de - si - o,

Ma non sò mai, ma non sò mai, ma _____

_____ non sò mai can-giar de - si - o,

*Fine*

31

Sem-pre l'i-stes-so sa-rà il mio fo - co,

35

Sem-pre l'i-stes-so sa-rà il mio fo - co, e sa-rò sem-pre l'i-

38

stes-so an-ch'i - o, e sa-rò sem-pre, e sa-rò sem -

42

*Da Capo al Fine*

-pre l'i-stes-so an-ch'i - o, __ l'i-stes-so an-ch'i - o.

*Da Capo al Fine*

*Always the same will be my love,/ and I shall be the same, too.*

145

# My Lovely Celia

Anonymous
*Altered by H. Lane Wilson, 1899, and J. G. P.*

George Monro

Notes about this song are on page 266.

kind,     And     with _____ your _ love ___ you'll ease _ my     mind.

charms;     O     take _____ me, _ dy - ing, to __ your     arms.

# My Lovely Celia

Anonymous
*Altered by H. Lane Wilson, 1899, and J. G. P.*

George Monro

Notes about this song are on page 266.

148

kind,     And  with _____ your \_ love \_\_\_\_\_ you'll  ease \_ my    mind.

charms;    O  take _____ me, \_  dy  -  ing,  to \_ your    arms.

# Sigh No More, Ladies

William Shakespeare

Richard J. S. Stevens
*Arranged by J. L. Hatton and E. Faning*

**Allegretto**

Sigh no more, la - dies, la - dies, sigh no more, ___
Sing no more, la - dies, la - dies, sing no more ___ Of

Men were de-ceiv - ers ev - er, men were de-ceiv - ers ev - er;
dumps so ___ dull and heav - y, of dumps so ___ dull and heav - y;

One foot in sea and one ___ on shore, ___ To
The fraud of men was ev - er so, ___ Since

Notes about this song are on page 266.

150

one thing con-stant nev - er, to one＿ thing＿ con-stant nev - er.)
sum-mer first was leav - y, since sum - mer＿ first was leav - y.)

Then sigh not so, but let them go, And be you blithe and＿

bon - ny, and be you＿ blithe and＿ bon - ny, Con - vert - ing＿ all your＿

sounds of＿ woe, con - vert - ing＿ all your＿ sounds of＿ woe To hey non - ny,

ten. mf

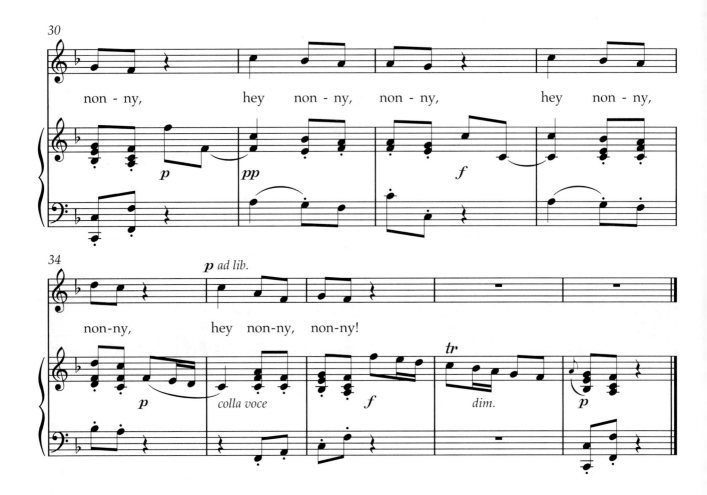

non - ny,     hey   non - ny,    non - ny,     hey    non - ny,

non-ny,     hey non-ny,   non-ny!

# Nel cor più non mi sento

Giuseppe Palomba

Giovanni Paisiello
*Arranged and edited by J. G. P.*

*(Text for a female singer:)* Nel cor più non mi sen - to Bril-lar la gio-ven-tù; Ca-
*(Text for a male singer:)* Ti sen - to, sì, ti sen - to, Bel fior di gio-ven-tù; Ca-

gion del mio tor-men - to A - mor, sei col - pa tu.) Mi stuz - zi-chi, mi
gion del mio tor-men - to, A-ni-ma mia, sei tu.)

*Literal translation: (Female) In my heart I no longer feel/ the brightness of youth./ The cause of my torment?/ Love, you are guilty./*
*(Male) I hear you, yes, I hear you,/ beautiful flower of youth!/ The cause of my torment?/ My soul, you are it/*

Notes about this song are on pages 266 and 276.

(Female) You pick on me, bite me,/ prick me, pinch me—/ what is all this?/ Pity, pity!/ Love is certain
(Male) You pick on me, bite me,/ prick me, pinch me—/ what is all this?/ Pity, pity!/ That face has a certain
(Both) something/ that makes me rave!

The solo version of "Nel cor . . ." ends with m. 28; it may be repeated with ornamentation. For the duet used in the opera, a female sings the first stanza, a male sings the second stanza, and after the second (m. 29), both singers sing the duet conclusion.

# Bitten

### Prayer

Christian Fürchtegott Gellert
*Translation by V. A. C. and J. G. P.*

Ludwig van Beethoven

**Feierlich und mit Andacht**
*Solemnly, and with devotion*

Gott, dei - ne Gü - te reicht _ so weit, So weit die
O God, your good - ness reach - es far, As far as

Wol - ken ge - hen; Du krönst uns mit Barm - her - zig -
clouds a - bove us; Your love ac - cepts us as we

*Literal translation: God, your goodness reaches/ as far as the clouds./ You crown us with your mercy/*
Notes about this song are on pages 267 and 281.

156

*and hurry to support us./ Lord, my fortress, my rock, my protection,/ hear my pleading, heed my words,/ because I want to pray to you.*

# Bitten

Prayer

Christian Fürchtegott Gellert
*Translation by V. A. C. and J. G. P.*

Ludwig van Beethoven

**Feierlich und mit Andacht**
*Solemnly, and with devotion*

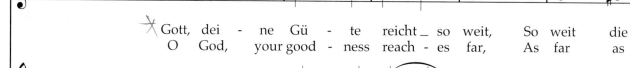

Gott, dei - ne Gü - te reicht _ so weit, So weit die
O God, your good - ness reach - es far, As far as

Wol - ken ge - hen; Du krönst uns mit Barm - her - zig-
clouds a - bove us; Your love ac - cepts us as we

*Literal translation: God, your goodness reaches/ as far as the clouds./ You crown us with your mercy/*

Notes about this song are on pages 267 and 281.

*and hurry to support us./ Lord, my fortress, my rock, my protection,/ hear my pleading, heed my words,/ because I want to pray to you.*

# An die Musik

## To Music

Franz von Schober

*Translation by J. G. P.*

Franz Schubert

*Literal translation: (1) You lovely art, in how many gray hours/ when life's wildness entrapped me,/*
*(2) Often a sigh escaped from your harp,/ a sweet, holy chord of yours,/*

Notes about this song are on pages 267 and 281.

*(1) have you fired my heart with warm love and lifted me to a better world!*
*(2) has opened a heaven of better times for me:/ you lovely art, I thank you for that!*

161

# An die Musik

## To Music

Franz von Schober
*Translation by J. G. P.*

Franz Schubert

*Literal translation: (1) You lovely art, in how many gray hours/ when life's wildness entrapped me,/*
*(2) Often a sigh escaped from your harp,/ a sweet, holy chord of yours,/*

Notes about this song are on pages 267 and 281.

(1) have you fired my heart with warm love and lifted me to a better world!
(2) has opened a heaven of better times for me:/ you lovely art, I thank you for that!

# Wanderers Nachtlied

## (Wanderer's Night Song)

Johann Wolfgang von Goethe

Franz Schubert

*Literal translation: Over all the mountain-peaks/ is peace,/ in all the tree-tops/ you can hardly hear a stir;/ the birds are silent,/*

Notes about this song are on pages 268 and 282.

8

schwei-gen im _ Wal - de. War-te nur, war-te nur! Bal - de Ruh-est du
si - lent their _ day - song. On - ly wait, on - ly wait, Ere _ long you will rest

11

auch. War-te nur, war-te nur! Bal - de Ru - hest du auch.
too. On - ly wait, on - ly wait! Ere _ long you will rest, too.

*are silent in the woods. Just wait—soon/ you will rest, too.*

*(Low Key)*

# Wanderers Nachtlied

## (Wanderer's Night Song)

Johann Wolfgang von Goethe                                                Franz Schubert

**Langsam** *(Slowly)*

Ü - ber al - len Gip - feln Ist
O - ver all the hill - tops is

*Literal translation: Over all the mountain-peaks/ is*

Notes about this song are on pages 268 and 282.

*peace,/ in all the tree-tops/ you can hardly hear a stir;/ the birds are silent,/ are silent in the woods. Just wait—soon/ you will rest, too.*

# A Red, Red Rose

Robert Burns

Robert Schumann

**Andantine**

O my luve_ is like a red,_ red rose, That's new - ly sprung in

June:_____ O my luve_ is like the mel - o-die, That's sweet - ly played in

tune.____ As fair art thou, my bo - nie lass, So deep in luve am

Notes about this song are on page 268.

I; _____ And I will luve thee still, my dear, Till a' the seas gang dry. Till a' the seas gang dry, my dear, And the rocks melt wi' the sun; _____And I \_ will luve thee still, my dear, While the sands o' life shall run. And fare thee weel, my

# A Red, Red Rose

*(Low Key)*

Robert Burns

Robert Schumann

Notes about this song are on page 268.

171

# Widmung

## Dedication

Wolfgang Müller
*Translation by J. G. P.*

Robert Franz

*Literal translation: O, do not say thanks for these songs—/ it is fitting for me to thank you!/ You gave them to me; I am giving back/ what now is and always was and will be yours.*

Notes about this song are on pages 268 and 282.

*Yes, they were all yours;/ from the light of your dear eyes/ I read them faithfully. Do you not recognize your own songs?*

*(Low Key)*

# Widmung
## Dedication

Wolfgang Müller
*Translation by J. G. P.*

Robert Franz

O danke nicht für die - se Lie - der, Mir ziemt es
*O do not thank me for my sing - ing; I am so*

dank-bar dir zu sein; Du gabst sie mir, Ich ge - be
*thank - ful for these songs! From you they came, I am re -*

wie - der, Was jetzt und einst und e - wig Dein.
*turn - ing The gift that still to you be - longs.*

*Literal translation: O, do not say thanks for these songs—/ it is fitting for me to thank you!! You gave them to me; I am giving back/ what now is and always was and will be yours.*

Notes about this song are on pages 268 and 282.

*Yes, they were all yours;/ from the light of your dear eyes/ I read them faithfully. Do you not recognize your own songs?*

# Some Folks

Stephen Foster

Stephen Foster

1. Some folks like to sigh,
2. Some folks get grey hairs,
3. Some folks toil and save,

Some folks do, some folks do;

Some folks long to die,
Brood-ing o'er their cares,
To buy them-selves a grave,

But that's not me nor

Notes about this song are on page 268.

you.     Long    live    the   mer-ry, mer-ry heart That   laughs by   night and

day,      Like the   Queen    of     mirth,      No    mat-ter what some folks

say.

# Some Folks

Stephen Foster

Stephen Foster

1. Some folks like to sigh,
2. Some folks get grey hairs,
3. Some folks toil and save,

Some folks do, some folks do;
Some folks long to die,
Brood-ing o'er their cares,
To buy them-selves a grave,
But that's not me nor

Notes about this song are on page 268.

# Santa Lucia

Teodoro Cottrau

Teodoro Cottrau

*Literal translation: (1) On the sea shines a silver star; calm are the waves, favorable the wind.*
*(2)With this breeze so gentle, how lovely it is to be on a boat!*

Notes about this song are on pages 269 and 276.

# Santa Lucia

Teodoro Cottrau

Teodoro Cottrau

*Literal translation: (1) On the sea shines a silver star; calm are the waves, favorable the wind.*
*(2)With this breeze so gentle, how lovely it is to be on a boat!*

Notes about this song are on pages 269 and 276.

# E l'uccellino

Renato Fucini

Giacomo Puccini

*Literal translation: And the little bird sings on the branch: Sleep peacefully, little dear. Lay down your*
Notes about this song are on pages 269 and 277.

*fair head on mama's heart. And the little bird sings on the twig: So many nice things you will learn, but if you want to know how much I*

*love you, no one on earth can ever say it. And the little bird sings to the bright sky: Sleep, my treasure, here on my bosom.*

# The Sky Above the Roof

Paul Verlaine  
*Translated by Mabel Dearmer*

Ralph Vaughan Williams

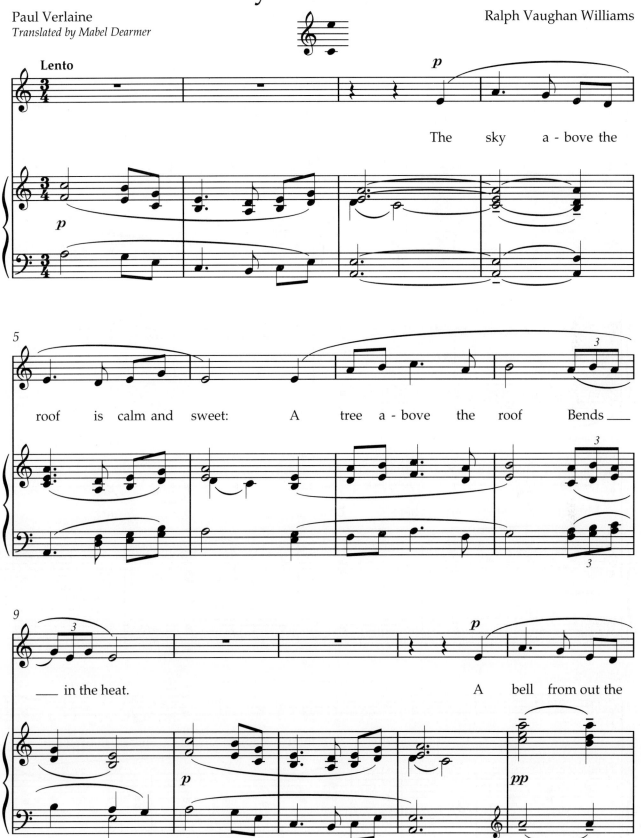

The sky a - bove the roof is calm and sweet: A tree a - bove the roof Bends in the heat. A bell from out the

Notes about this song are on page 269.

tears? What hast thou done, O heart, _____ With thy spent_

years? _____

# At the River

Robert R. Lowry

Robert R. Lowry
*Arranged by Charles Ives*

x

Shall we gath-er at the riv - er,

Where bright an - gel feet have trod, _____ With its crys - tal tide for -

From: *Thirty Four Songs.* © 1933 Merion Music Inc. Reprinted By Permission Of The Publisher.

Notes about this song are on page 269.

x

190

Note: At the end of measure 13 Ives placed an eighth rest with a fermata, creating a measure of 13/8 time. The marking used here is called a *caesura* and indicates complete silence.

# By the Sea

Roger Quilter

Roger Quilter

Notes about this song are on page 269.

194

20

stood      to - day   by the   shim - m'ring   sea; _____   Nev - er was

22

wind _____   so   mild __ and   free; _____   The

24

light and the   love - li - ness daz - zled   me, _____   daz -   zled

27

me.

(High Key)

# To a Brown Girl, Dead

Countee Cullen

Margaret Bonds

Notes about this song are on page 270.

*(Low Key)*

# To a Brown Girl, Dead

Countee Cullen

Margaret Bonds

Notes about this song are on page 270.

198

Death has found her sweet. _____ Her moth-er pawned her wed-ding ring _____ To lay her out _ in white. _____ She'd be so proud she'd dance and sing To see her-self _____ to - night. _____

# Ain't Misbehavin'

Andy Razaf                                    Thomas Waller and Harry Brooks

Boy: Tho' it's a fick-le age    With flirt-ing all the rage,
Girl: Your type of man is rare,    I know you real-ly care.

Here is one bird with self-con-trol,    Hap-py in-side my cage.
That's why my con-science nev-er sleeps    When you're a-way some-where.

Notes about this song are on page 270.

I know who I love best,
Sure was a luck-y day

Thumbs down to all the rest;
When fate sent you my way

My love was giv-en, heart and soul, __
And made you mine a-lone for keeps, __

So it can stand the test.
Dit-to to all you say.

*Chorus*
*Slowly, with expression*

No one to talk with, all by my self,

No one to walk with, but

I'm hap-py on __ the shelf,

Ain't mis-be-hav-in',

I'm sav-in' my love for

Your kiss - es are worth wait - ing for, Be - lieve me.

I don't stay out late, don't care to go, I'm home a-bout eight, just

me and my ra - di - o, Ain't mis-be-hav-in', I'm sav-in' my love for

you. you.

*(High Key)*

# Love Is Here to Stay

Ira Gershwin

George Gershwin

Notes about this song are on page 270.

Not for a year, But ev - er and a day.

The ra - di - o and the tel - e-phone and the mov-ies that we

know May just be pass-ing fan - cies, And in time may go.

But, oh my dear, Our love is here to stay;

206

Lyrics under the music:

To - geth - er we're go - ing a long, long way.

In time the Rock-ies may crum-ble, Gib - ral - ter may tum-ble,

They're on - ly made of clay, But our love is here to

1. stay. _____ It's ver - y    2. stay. _____

*(Low Key)*

# Love Is Here to Stay

Ira Gershwin

George Gershwin

**Con anima**

*mp* *cresc.*     *cresc.*     *mf*

The more I read the pa - pers The less I com - pre -

*mp*
*leggiero*

hend The world and all its ca - pers And how it all will

Notes about this song are on page 270.

# A Cockeyed Optimist

Oscar Hammerstein II

Richard Rodgers

Notes about this song are on page 270.

So they call me a cock - eyed op - ti - mist,_____ Im-ma-
But I'm on - ly a cock - eyed op - ti - mist,_____ And I

ture and in - cur - a - bly green!_____ I have
can't get it in - to my

head._____ I hear the hu - man race is

fall-ing on its face And has-n't ver - y far to go,_____

*poco rit.*    *a tempo*

213

But ev-'ry whip-poor-will is sell-ing me a bill, And tell-ing me it just ain't so. _____ I could say life is just a bowl of jel-lo, _____ And ap-pear more in-tel-li-gent and smart, _____ But I'm stuck (like a

dope!) with a thing called hope, And I can't get it
out of my heart, _____ Not _____
this _____ heart. _____

*poco a poco cresc.*

(High Key)

# One Hand, One Heart

Stephen Sondheim

Leonard Bernstein

Notes about this song are on page 270.

Make of our lives one life. Day af-ter day one

life. Now it be - gins, now we start; One hand,

one heart. E - ven death won't part_____ us now._____

now.

(Low Key)

# One Hand, One Heart

Stephen Sondheim

Leonard Bernstein

Notes about this song are on page 270.

Make of our lives one life. Day af-ter day one

life. Now it be - gins, now we start; One hand,

one heart. E - ven death won't part_____ us now._____

now.

# I'll Know

Frank Loesser

Frank Loesser

Notes about this song are on page 270.

care,   how I care,   how I   care.          And I'll  stop,                     and I'll

stare,                    And I'll know          long be - fore   we can speak, I'll

know          in my   heart.          I'll     know          and I

won't ev - er ask,     "Am I   right,    am I wise,    am I smart?"          But I'll

stop          and I'll stare          at that face          in the

throng:          Yes, I'll know          when my love          comes a -

long.          I'll          long.

# Soon It's Gonna Rain

Tom Jones

Harvey Schmidt

Notes about this song are on page 271.

Now is the time to run in-side and stay.

Now is the time to find a hide-a-

way Where we can stay.

*colla voce*          *mp* *a tempo*

Ad lib          Moderato

*p*

Soon it's gon-na rain. What-'ll we do with you____

We'll find four limbs of a tree. We'll

build four walls and a floor. We'll bind it

o - ver with leaves And run in - side to stay.

47 _a tempo_

Then we'll let it rain; We'll not feel it. Then we'll let it rain;

50

Rain pell - mell. And we'll not com-plain If it nev-er stops at

53

all. _____ We'll live and love with-

56 _rall._ _a tempo_

in our own four walls. _____

# Make Someone Happy

Betty Comden and Adolph Green

Jule Styne

Make _____ some-one hap - py, make just one ___ some-one hap - py,

Make just one ___ heart the heart you sing to.

Notes about this song are on page 271.

# Far From the Home I Love

Sheldon Harnick

Jerry Bock

Lyrics:

How can I hope to make you un-der-stand Why I do what I do?

Why I must trav-el to a dis-tant land, Far from the home I love.

Notes about this song are on page 271.

## Yesterday

John Lennon and Paul McCartney

John Lennon and Paul McCartney

I must go. Who could im-ag-ine I'd be wan-d'ring so

Far from the home I love? Yet there with my love I'm home.

Moderately, with expression

Yes-ter-day
Sud-den-ly,

Notes about this song are on page 271.

all my trou-bles seemed so far ___ a - way, ___
I'm not half ___ the man ___ I used to be, _____

Now it ___ looks ___ as though ___ they're here to stay, _ Oh,
There's a shad - ow hang-ing o - ver me, ___ Oh

I be - lieve ___ in yes - ter - day. ___
yes - ter - day ___ came sud - den - ly.

Why she had to go I don't know, she would-n't say. _

235

*Perform smaller notes the second time only.

# Happiness

Clark Gesner

Clark Gesner

Notes about this song are on page 271.

Ty - ing your shoe for the ver - y first time.
Shar-ing a sand - wich, _ get-ting a - long.

Hap - pi - ness is play - ing the drum in your own school
Hap - pi - ness is sing - ing to - geth - er when day is

band. And Hap - pi - ness is walk - ing hand in
through. And Hap - pi - ness is those who sing with

*(High Key)*

# Anyone Can Whistle

Stephen Sondheim

Stephen Sondheim

Notes about this song are on page 271.

# Anyone Can Whistle

Stephen Sondheim

Stephen Sondheim

**Slow and gentle**

An-y-one can whis-tle, that's what they say— Eas-y.

An - y - one can whis-tle, an - y old day— Eas - y.

Notes about this song are on page 271.

It's all so sim-ple: Re - lax, let go, let fly. So some-one tell me why can't I? I can dance a tan-go, I can read Greek— Eas-y I can slay a drag-on an-y old week— Eas-y.

What's hard is sim - ple, What's nat-u-ral comes hard. May - be you could show me how to let go, low - er my guard, learn to be free. May - be if you whis-tle, whis - tle for me.

# Believe in Yourself

Charlie Smalls

Charlie Smalls

Notes about this song are on page 271.

feel      and know you're right  be - cause      the time will come a-

round    when you'll say   it's  yours.          Be -

lieve there's a  rea-son    to   be,     be - lieve you can make time   stand

still;      and know from the mo-ment   you  try,     if

you be - lieve, _____ I know you will. _____

Be - lieve in your-self right from the start;

you'll have brains, you'll have a heart. You'll have cour-age to

last your whole life through, _____ if you be -

lieve in your-self, _____ if you be - lieve in your-self, _____

if you be - lieve in your-self as I be - lieve in

you. _____

rall.

# What I Did for Love

Edward Kleban

Marvin Hamlisch

Notes about this song are on page 271.

10

What I did for love, __ what I did for love. _____

13

Look my eyes _ are dry, _____ The gift was ours to

16

bor - row. _____ It's as if __ we al - ways

19

knew, _____ And I won't for-get __ What I did for love, _

what I did for love.

Gone, love is nev-er gone,

As we tra-vel on, Love's what we'll re-

mem - ber. Kiss to-day good-bye,

dim. mp

# The Greatest Love of All

Linda Creed

Michael Masser

Words by Linda Creed. Music by Michael Masser. © 1977 EMI Gold Horizon Music Corp. and EMI Golden Torch Music Corp. All Rights Reserved. Used by Permission. *Warner Bros. Publications U.S. Inc.*, Miami, FL 33014.

Notes about this song are on page 271.

me. I de-cid - ed long __ a - go __ nev-er to walk in an - y-one's shad-ow.

If I fail, __ if I suc - ceed, __ at least I've lived __ as I be - lieve. No

mat - ter what they take from me, they can't take a - way my dig - ni - ty.

Be-cause the great - est love of all __ is hap-pen-ing to

me. I found the great - est love of all _ in-side of

me. The great - est love _ of all _____ is ea - sy to a -

chieve. Learn-ing _ to love your-self, ___ it is the

great - est love of all. And if by chance that spe - cial place

that you've been dream-ing of

leads you to a

lone - ly _ place, find your strength in love. _____

# All I Ask of You

Charles Hart
Additional lyrics by Richard Stilgoe

Andrew Lloyd Webber

**Andante**

No more talk of dark-ness, for - get these wide-eyed fears; I'm

Notes about this song are on page 271.

here, noth-ing can harm you, my words will warm and calm you.

Let me be your free-dom, let day-light dry your tears; I'm

here, with you, be-side you, to guard you and to guide you.

All I ask is ev-'ry wak-ing mo-ment, turn my head with talk of

259

sum-mer-time.    Say    you need me with you now    and    al-ways;

prom-ise me    that all you say is    true,    Love me, that's all I ask of

you.

An-y-where you go, let me go    too;    love me, that's all I ask of    you.

# A Notes on the Songs

**Songs for group singing**

"**America the Beautiful,**" page 82, was inspired by the view from Pike's Peak. Katherine Lee Bates, professor of English at Wellesley College, wrote the words on the morning after climbing Pike's Peak during a Colorado vacation in 1893. The tune by Samuel A. Ward is somewhat older, 1882. The tune and words were published together in 1912.

"**De colores,**" page 82, a happy song about nature, is universally known and loved in Mexico.

"**Do-Re-Mi,**" page 83. Set in Austria in 1938, *The Sound of Music* is based on the true story of Maria Rainer, the young governess of seven children. She married their father and became Baroness Maria von Trapp. When the family escaped Nazi persecution by emigrating, she led the children into an international concert career as the Trapp Family Singers. Mary Martin proposed putting their story on stage, and she created the leading role.

"**Down in the Valley,**" page 83. This courting song is said to have come from the mountains of Kentucky. Carl Sandburg gave another version of this song in *The American Songbag* (New York, 1927) and referred to it as "an old lyric of English origin." Kurt Weill (1900–1950) used this tune in a one-act opera by the same name; it was the first opera ever telecast by the NBC Television Opera Theatre (1950).

"**He's Got the Whole World in His Hands,**" page 84. This song was first published in Edward Boatner's *Spirituals Triumphant* (Nashville, 1927.) The melody is given here as Marian Anderson sang it on a 1962 recording. Anderson, who was the greatest concert singer of her time and the first black artist ever to sing at the Metropolitan Opera, sang this spiritual at the historic rally in Washington, D.C., where Dr. Martin Luther King Jr. delivered his memorable "I Have a Dream" speech.

"**Let There Be Peace on Earth,**" page 85. Beginning in measure 16, the original words were "With God as our Father, Brothers all are we; let me walk with my brother . . ."

"**Michael, Row the Boat Ashore,**" page 86. In the Bible, Michael and Gabriel are named as angels. "Hallelujah" = praise God (Hebrew). In spirituals, crossing the Jordan River symbolizes going to a better place, either in death or in liberation.

"**Scarborough Fair,**" page 86, is a humorous song about a former sweetheart. You promise to be sweethearts again if she or he will do three tasks that, in fact, are quite impossible.

The tune was made famous by Paul Simon and Art Garfunkel, but many other versions also exist. The words given here were written down in 1891 from the singing of a fisherman from North Riding, Yorkshire, England. Mr. Moat sang two complete sets of words, one set appropriate for a woman and one for a man. Each set ends with this stanza:

> And now I have answered your questions three,
> I hope you'll answer as many for me.
> I hope you'll answer as many for me,
>     And then thou shalt be a true lover of mine.

This stanza is puzzling because there are no answers to the impossible challenges. These words and the melodies Mr. Moat sang are found in: *English Country Songs* by Lucy E. Broadwood and J. A. Fuller Maitland. London: Leadenhall Press, 1893.

**"Shalom Chaverim,"** page 87. This version has been adapted from one in *The Jewish Center Songster* (New York, 1949).

**"She'll Be Comin' Round the Mountain,"** page 87, was adapted by railroad work gangs from a negro spiritual, *"Oh, Who Will Drive the Chariot When She Comes."*

**"The Star-Spangled Banner,"** page 88. Francis Scott Key, district attorney for Washington, D.C., was on board a ship in Baltimore harbor, unable to land during the nighttime bombardment of Fort McHenry by the British in 1814. When morning light revealed that the fort had not surrendered, Key wrote this poem, expressing his pride. The tune is an English drinking song of the 1700s, *"To Anacreon in Heaven."* The United States had no official anthem until 1931, when this song was chosen. Lower notes (not part of the official anthem) are suggested here for those who are uncomfortable with the wide range of the song.

**"Viva la musica!",** page 89. Michael Praetorius (1571–1621) also wrote the Christmas song, *"Lo, How a Rose E'er Blooming."*

**"When the Saints Go Marchin' In,"** page 89, was copyrighted in 1896 by J. M. Black (tune) and Katharine E. Purvis (text) and was published in a gospel song collection by Ira B. Sankey. But there is doubt about the real origin of the song, which may have come from the Bahamas. Around 1900 jazz musicians supposedly played this song for funerals: slowly on the way to the cemetery and in fast tempo coming back. It has gone around the world as a spiritual; I heard it sung in Italy by nuns in a religious procession.

**Traditional songs**

**"Auprès de ma blonde,"** page 90, a lively song from northern France, celebrates the love of a happy young wife and husband. Notice that the bride's three verses all form one long sentence, interrupted by the man's refrain. This alternation means that anyone can sing this song, making it widely popular.

**"Cielito lindo,"** pages 92 and 94, is one of the most popular songs to come out of Mexico. Published versions go back to the 1920s, but the song is certainly much older.

**"Cockles and Mussels,"** pages 96 and 99. Burl Ives wrote about this song:
"To the north and to the south of the port of Dublin, there are wide stretches of sand, covered by shallow water at high water. Many a 'dacint poor woman' in other days earned an honest penny by harvesting cockles and mussels, which were to be found in great numbers on these sands, and selling them on the streets of Dublin." (*Irish Songs*, 1958)
Ives sang the refrain, measures 36–45, after each stanza.

**"Early One Morning,"** pages 102 and 104. William Chappell, an authority on English folk song, first published this old song in 1840, but he did not know its source. He wrote that this was one of the songs most often sung by domestic serving girls going about their work.

**"High Barbaree,"** page 106, refers to a battle with pirates along the coast of Barbary, the region of northern Africa between the Atlantic Ocean and Egypt's western border. Pirates ruled this part of the Mediterranean Sea throughout the 1700s. "Chanteys" were sung by sailors to the rhythm of their work. The word probably comes from French *chantez*, a command to "Sing!"

**"I Know Where I'm Going,"** page 108, a song from County Antrim in the northeast corner of Ireland, was written down and arranged by Herbert Hughes in *Irish Country Songs* in 1909. Hughes suggested that a male singer can add two notes to the first and last stanzas, singing "I know where I'm going, *she said, . . .*" Hughes explained that in Ulster dialect "dear knows" = goodness knows. A line in stanza 3 originally said "Some say he's black," meaning sullen or ungracious. This edition changes the phrase to make it understandable to modern listeners.

**"Love Will Find Out the Way,"** page 111. The tune, first published in 1652 in Playford's *Musick's Recreation*, was still current in England as a folk song in the 1800s. The words were published in 1765 in Percy's *Reliques of Ancient English Poetry*.

**"El Tecolote,"** page 114, is sung to children at bedtime. "Cu-cu-ri-cu" imitates the sound of the owl. "Tecolote de Guadiana" is a species of owl named after the Guadiana River in Spain. The optional lower part in parallel thirds gives a typically Mexican sound.

**"The Turtle Dove,"** page 116, is one of many English folk songs named after this gentle bird.

**"Walk Together, Children,"** page 118, was included in *Cabin and Plantation Songs*, 1874, as sung by students at the Hampton Institute (now Hampton University), Virginia. J. B. Towe described the origin of the song:

> This hymn was made by a company of Slaves, who were not allowed to sing or pray anywhere the old master could hear them. When he died, their old mistress looked on them with pity and granted them the privilege of singing and praying in the cabins at night. Then they sang this hymn and shouted for joy and gave God the honor and praise.

This story explains why mourning (for the death of the old master) is mixed with the happiness of those who have received permission to worship as they wish. No wonder the "mourning" of the slaves was so joyful, if their old owner had forbidden them to worship!

"Promised Land" refers to Heaven.

This edition gives the melody as it was published by two eminent black authorities. In 1917 J. Rosamond Johnson made a concert arrangement of this "Triumphant Negro Marching Song" and recommended tom-toms and drums in the accompaniment. He used one verse and refrain and another verse and refrain with a slightly extended ending. R. Nathaniel Dett also published a version for solo and choir, singing alternately. He suggested singing the verse three times, using "walk," "talk," and "sing" in succession, before going on to sing the refrain once.

I do not recommend singing black dialect unless it comes naturally to you. An exception: The word "tire" has two syllables in the refrain; everyone should sing "ti-ah."

# Art songs and arias

## The Renaissance period

Most of the artistic music composed during the Renaissance was choral music for church use. At the very end of the Renaissance, in Elizabethan England, new techniques in music printing and a new level of prosperity led to a flood of new songs for voice and lute. No other period has known so many good composers who wrote both poetry and music.

**"It Was a Lover and His Lass,"** pages 120 and 123, may have been written especially for a Shakespearean play. Thomas Morley (1557–1602) and Shakespeare (1564–1616) were neighbors for a time in London and were undoubtedly acquainted. Morley was organist at St. Paul's Cathedral and a musician at the court of Elizabeth I.

The song occurs near the end of *As You Like It,* sung by two page boys for the amusement of a clown and his bride-to-be. The scene contains some clever comments on amateur singing. "Cornfield" = wheat field, "ringtime" = wedding season.

The original printed music was meant to be laid on a table between two or more performers. The lutenist-singer read it from one side of the table while a string bass player read the bass part from the other side. Below the voice part are lute tablature symbols, alphabet letters arranged along horizontal lines that represent the lute's six strings (tuned G-c-f-a-d'-g'). Each letter indicates a fret where the string should be stopped, and further symbols indicate rhythm. This system makes clear exactly what notes to play, including the interesting chromatic changes.

Performance: Imagine the bridal couple dancing and keep the tempo moving. In the changing meters at measures 25 and 26, keep the quarter-notes moving evenly, and put stresses where the words require them. Elizabethan composers often used tricks like this to keep their rhythms lively.

Accompaniment: Morley asked for lute and bass viol; guitar and cello would be next best. This edition gives voice and bass parts exactly as Morley wrote them; harmonies are adapted so that the pianist doubles the singer's notes.

Source: *First Booke of Ayres* (London, 1600), reproduced in facsimile in *English Lute Songs*, Vol. 8, No. 33. Meter: Alla breve. Key: G major with no signature. Voice part in G clef, beginning on g1. Shakespeare's poem has four stanzas.

**"When Laura Smiles,"** page 126, has both words and music by Philip Rosseter (1568?–1623). Let a bright tempo swing the song along cheerfully. This lover speaks of sorrow and despair, but only to say that Laura's smile takes them away. In the double-length measures (15 and 22), keep the quarter-notes equal.

In the first edition, the page layout was like that described for "It Was a Lover and His Lass," except for being all on one page.

Accompaniment: The same as for Morley's song. If a piano is used, the pianist should play the lowest notes as lightly as possible and use little or no pedal.

Source: *A Booke of Ayres* (1601), reproduced in facsimile in *English Lute Songs*, Vol. 9, No. 36. Meter: 3. Key: G major with no signature. (The third note in measures 6 and 10 has no accidental but probably a raised leading tone is assumed.) The first stanza of the text is printed under the music; three more stanzas are printed at the foot of the page. This edition uses stanzas 1 and 4. All stanzas are given in *An Anthology of Elizabethan Lute Songs, Madrigals, and Rounds* edited by Noah Greenberg, W. H. Auden, and Chester Kallman.

**"Since First I Saw Your Face,"** pages 128 and 130. Thomas Ford (15??–1648) was a musician at the royal court in London.

Accompaniment: The voice and bass parts given here are authentic, but the harmonization is adapted to the piano from the original for lute.

Source: *Musick of Sundrie Kindes* (London, 1607). Key: C. The lute tablature is also reproduced in *Ten Airs* edited by Fellowes and Dart. Stainer & Bell, London, 1966.

*The Baroque period*

A new musical language, the Baroque style, was born in Italy at about the same time as the English songs described above were bringing the Renaissance to a close. The Baroque style grew out of the dramatic needs of the newly invented opera, a play sung throughout, with music intensifying every word of the poetic text. Usually recognized as the first opera was *Euridice* by Jacopo Peri, performed in Florence, Italy, in 1600 on the occasion of a royal wedding.

The new feature of opera was an accompaniment with slow chords over which the singer had the utmost freedom to sing words expressively, not being bound to a steady rhythm. Single notes in the bass part indicated the chords, which were filled in by players who improvised on keyboard or fretted instruments. Because the bass was constantly present, we call it the *basso continuo*; and the interaction of the melody and bass parts became the identifying mark of Baroque style.

**"Man Is for the Woman Made,"** pages 132 and 134, is a lively comic song by Henry Purcell (1659–1695), the greatest English composer. His opera *Dido and Aeneas* is still performed often, but he wrote songs for many plays that are no longer done. This song was sung in Thomas Scott's comedy *The Mock Marriage*, 1695. Peter Anthony Motteux, a music journalist and a friend of Purcell's, wrote the words.

Accompaniment: In the Baroque era harpsichord and bass viol were normally used; the bass part is the same as that of the piano part. Use no pedal; let the chords be detached when appropriate. The chords have been filled in by the editor; feel free to change them as you like.

No primary source is available, but the first measures are given in Zimmermann's catalog of Purcell's works. For voice (treble clef, starting on c2) and continuo. Key: C. Meter: alla breve. Text: *Wit and Mirth, or Pills to Purge Melancholy* (1720), Vol. III. Stanza 3, line 4, originally read "Whore, bawd or harridan. . . ."

**"Dolce scherza,"** pages 136 and 138. Giacomo Antonio Perti (1661–1754) was a prominent composer and teacher in Bologna, Italy.

Accompaniment: The style is the same as in the song by Purcell.

Source: No primary source is available. A romanticized version of this aria appeared in *Bel Canto* (Braunschweig, c1900) by Albert Fuchs, who found it in the State Library of Dresden, Germany. The original was stolen in World War II but may still exist in Russia. Using Fuchs's version, I have tried to guess what the original may be like.

**"Vado ben spesso,"** pages 140 and 143. This jaunty song is sung by a person who is on the go, which describes the life of Giovanni Bononcini (1670–1747). Born in Modena, Italy, he was George Frideric Handel's chief competitor for a while in London, but he ended his career in Vienna.

This song brings up several terms that one often reads in music history. We call it an *aria* (air) mainly because that is the Italian word most often used for accompanied songs. It does not come from an *opera*, which is staged in a theater, nor from an *oratorio*, which is performed without staging in a church or a concert hall. It comes from a *solo cantata*, a piece meant to be sung by one singer at home, in a voice studio, or at the home of a wealthy person who can afford to hire professional musicians to entertain. *"Vado ben spesso"* is the first of three arias in the cantata.

This aria is longer than it looks. At the end of measure 46, you are instructed to go back to the beginning and start over *da capo*, "from the top." *Da capo arias* were easy to write but also popular with audiences. Why? First, a good tune is worth hearing twice. Also, repetition allows the singer to show off by adding ornaments to the melody, in somewhat the same way as a jazz player improvises on a popular song. A quick tune like this one does not need many ornaments, but some are suggested here in small notes; try them out and then feel free to make up your own.

Accompaniment: The same as for the preceding two songs.

Source: British Library Additional Ms. 14, 211, and Milano Conservatory Ms. Noseda C-65-7. The British manuscript gives the higher version of measure 27; the Milano manuscript gives the lower version. For voice (soprano clef) and continuo. Key: D. Meter: alla breve.

Franz Liszt quoted this aria in *"Années de Pèlerinage,"* a set of piano pieces. He and others in the 1800s believed wrongly that the composer was Salvator Rosa, a famous painter.

**"My Lovely Celia,"** pages 146 and 148, is typical of popular songs in London during Handel's time. Although little is known about George Monro (1680–1731), his well-liked song was reprinted several times during the 1700s.

There are two versions of the anonymous poem. The original version compared Celia to the gods of Greece. Here are two stanzas of the original five; you may sing them if you prefer. "Fresh alarms" = "new calls to battle."

> My goddess Celia, heav'nly fair,
> As lilies sweet, so soft as air;
> Let loose thy tresses, spread thy charms,
> And to my love give fresh alarms.
>
> O let me gaze on those bright eyes,
> Tho' sacred lightning from 'em flies:
> Thou art all over endless charms!
> O take me, dying, to thy arms.

H. Lane Wilson, probably feeling that the original text, containing the word "goddess," was unacceptable, wrote *"My Lovely Celia,"* which has become well known. I have adjusted Lane's words to remove extra syllables from lines 3 and 4.

Performance: Bring the song to life with the smooth, stately rhythms of the minuet. When you sing Celia's name, add an ornament to the note to make it special. The printed sign is "tr," meaning trill, but a grace note or any other ornament will do as well. For the poetic meter "heav'n" is contracted into one syllable, but you may pronounce the syllable -ven on the fourth eighth-note to make the word clearer.

When one syllable carries over several notes, sing as smoothly as you can. Also enjoy your chance to soar up without accompaniment on the word "more." A singer of the 1700s would certainly put a trill on the half-note in measure 19, beginning one note above the printed note.

Accompaniment: The introduction is optional; it is not part of the original song. The style is the same as for the preceding four songs.

Source: *Musical Miscellany*, Vol. IV, pp. 124–25. Watts, London, 1730. Copy in the Library of Congress, Washington, D.C. For voice (treble clef, starting on d2) and continuo. Key: G. Meter: 3/4. Heading: "Set by Mr. G. MONRO," which implies that some other person wrote the poem. Stanza 1 printed with the notes, stanzas 2–5 on the opposite page.

## The classical period

As the Classical style developed in the works of J. S. Bach's sons and the works of Haydn, the piano became many composers' favorite instrument because it was stronger and more expressive than the harpsichord. Musicians gave up the Baroque custom of improvising keyboard accompaniments over a *basso continuo* and used fully written out accompaniments, both for keyboard and for orchestra.

**"Sigh No More, Ladies,"** page 150, comes from Shakespeare's *Much Ado About Nothing*, Act II:3. Richard John Samuel Stevens (1757–1837) composed it as a *glee*, a song for several voices; but it has been sung as a solo in many productions of the play.

Source: *Songs of England*, edited by J. L. Hatton and Eaton Faning, London, no date.

**"Nel cor più non mi sento,"** page 153, expresses a temporary case of lovesickness felt by a young woman, Rachelina, who is usually very lively. Her wooer, Coloandro, repeats her song with slightly different words, and then their voices join in a gentle complaint about this love that is causing them so much trouble.

Rachelina is the heroine of *La Molinara (The Lady Mill Owner)*, a comic opera written in 1788 by Giovanni Paisiello (1740–1816). Her aria was a concert favorite of many great sopranos, but it is only the first part of the duet. In the comic scene that follows, Coloandro goes into hiding; Rachelina sings her song again; and another man, also in love with her, shows up and joins in her song to make it a duet again.

This arrangement can be done several ways: (1) as a solo for female or male voice (measures 1–28), with or without the postlude (measures 41–44); (2) as a solo, singing the aria twice and varying it the second time; or (3) the original version, with the repeat sung by the male and continuing to the duet portion in measure 29 to the end.

Source: *Antologia Classica Musicale,* Anno IV, no. 4 (1845), Milano: G. Ricordi. Full score, Florence: A. Rocchi, 1962. For soprano, tenor, and small orchestra. Original key: G. Beethoven wrote a set of piano variations on this aria.

**"Bitten,"** pages 156 and 158, shows how simply one of the greatest composers of all time could write. Ludwig van Beethoven (1770–1827) composed it in 1803, the same year as his Symphony No. 3, the magnificent *"Eroica."*

Beethoven probably meant his "Six Songs of Gellert" to be sung at home. German sacred songs were not used in the Roman Catholic churches of Austria, and there were still not many public concerts that featured songs. The poems, written by Christian Fuerchtegott Gellert (1715–1769), were widely known and had been set to music earlier by C. P. E. Bach, one of the musical sons of the great J. S. Bach.

Performance: Beethoven loved singers and singing, but he demanded the utmost of all performers. Even this brief song has one strenuous passage (measures 27–32), where the voice stays on one pitch in the upper part of the voice. Be sure to breathe often enough, even at every comma, to stay physically free. Notice that measure 33 is suddenly soft after a long crescendo; Beethoven liked this effect and used it also in measures 15 and 36.

Accompaniment: Notice how often Beethoven used slurs in the left hand, indicating that the bass should sound melodic and interesting.

Source: *Sechs Lieder von Gellert,* Opus 48, no. 1. (1803) Key: E. Tempo marking: "Feierlich und mit Andacht."

*The Romantic period*   The 1800s, which began with the tumult of the Napoleonic Wars, brought radical changes into the lives of Europeans. The breakdown of old monarchies led to rebelliousness among students and intellectuals. Individual freedoms took on new importance, and individual emotions became the focus of a new artistic movement, Romanticism. There was great poverty (think of Dickens's *A Christmas Carol*) and pervasive social injustice. At the same time, industrialization also produced a growing middle class. A piano in the family's parlor was an acknowledged symbol of financial stability.

**"An die Musik,"** pages 160 and 162, glows with happiness as it expresses thanks to music, which meant everything to Franz Schubert (1797–1828). Like Beethoven, Schubert supported himself as a composer, but he did not have the advantage of Beethoven's fame as a piano virtuoso. He lived in poverty, often supported by his friends, until his early death.

No friend did more for young Schubert, jobless at age 20, than Franz von Schober (1796–1882), the poet of this song. After Schubert quit teaching at his father's school, Schober gave him food and lodging, opera tickets, and music paper and introduced him to a famous singer named Vogl, who made Schubert's songs known in the musical circles of Vienna.

Schubert's works are known by their numbers in the catalog compiled by O. E. Deutsch. This song is D.547, which means that it is estimated to be Schubert's 547th work.

Performance: Many singers take this song too slowly and with a melancholy attitude; remember that it was written by two young men, whose "better world" lay in their dreams for the future. The tempo marking is "moderate," and the meter signature shows that there are only two beats to a measure, so the tempo moves along cheerfully. Practice the high notes in measures 13 and 16 carefully to keep them in tempo. While you sing, listen to the wonderful melodic bass part in the pianist's left hand; think of your melody as a duet with the bass melody.

The original notation used two unusual appoggiaturas, which are shown in this edition not as Schubert wrote them as they should be sung. The first note of measure 5 was originally a small eighth-note slurred to a normal dotted quarter. The first note of measure 17 was a small quarter slurred to a normal half.

Accompaniment: Throughout the song, the left hand is more important than the right; notice the careful articulation markings that Schubert provided. Only in measures 19–23 does the right hand provide a contrast to the bass; the accents in these measures probably imply a slight lingering on the dissonant, accented chords.

Source: *Du holde Kunst*, D.547 (March 1817). Key: D. Tempo: *Mässig*.

**"Wanderers Nachtlied,"** pages 164 and 165, is one of the most loved poems in German literature. It was written in 1780 on the wall of a mountain cabin in Thuringia, Germany, by Johann Wolfgang von Goethe (1749–1832), the author of "Faust" and beyond question the greatest German poet.

Franz Peter Schubert learned the Classical style from singing as a boy soprano in the choir of the Imperial Chapel and from composition lessons with Antonio Salieri. Poetry led him to Romanticism, which emphasized personal feelings and love of nature, two qualities expressed in this song.

Performance: Quietness is all around, says the poem, and the music adds a sense of wonderment to the scene. You, too, will rest, says the poem, and the music adds a sense of deep satisfaction. The dynamic level is soft throughout, swelling a little at the climaxes in measures 10 and 12. Be sure, however, to use enough tone to be heard clearly and to have a good quality.

Source: *Wanderers Nachtlied*, D. 768. Key: B♭. Tempo: Langsam.

**"A Red, Red Rose,"** pages 167 and 169, is a simple love song with lyrics written by Robert Burns (1759–1796). The Romantics honored Burns as a genuine poet of the people; his poems were translated and widely read in Germany. Robert Schumann (1810–1856) wrote the melody in March 1840, six months before his marriage to Clara Wieck (the story of their romance makes good reading). The original Scots words fit Schumann's music with slight changes. "A' the seas gang . . ." = all the seas go.

Source: *Fünf Lieder und Gesänge*, Opus 27, no. 2. Original key: A.

**"Widmung,"** pages 172 and 174, takes us to the heart of Romanticism, the artistic movement that put the expression of personal emotions ahead of every other consideration. Robert Franz (1815–1892) lived a quiet life and favored serenity in music as well, but his songs are both sincere and original.

Source: *Lieder*, Opus 14, no. 1.

**"Some Folks,"** pages 176 and 178 expresses an unbeatable determination to be happy. Stephen Collins Foster (Pittsburgh, 1826; New York City, 1864) needed this determination to make his way as a song writer. His earlier songs, written for minstrel shows, are marred by racial stereotypes; but later Foster abandoned Negro dialect and broadened his subject matter. His 200 songs have been published in many kinds of arrangements, none of which are as clear, tasteful, and correct as Foster's original versions.

Source: "Some Folks." Firth & Pond, New York, 1855. Key: F.

**"Santa Lucia,"** pages 180 and 182, known all over the world as an Italian folk song, was written in 1850 by Teodoro Cottrau (1827–1879), a music publisher in Naples. The waterfront of old Naples lies within the parish of the church of St. Lucia (Lucy). In this song a sailor invites us to ride to Naples in his boat.

Source: *Songs of Italy* (London: before 1900?). Key: D♭.

*The Modern period* Around 1900 many musicians believed that composers like Wagner and Strauss had stretched conventional ways of composing to the breaking point and that completely new ways had to be found. Charles Ives was one of the searchers, but he worked alone, unknown to other musicians. Igor Stravinsky, Paul Hindemith, and Béla Bartók were among the international musicians who found new paths and influenced the new music of the twentieth century.

**"E l'uccellino,"** page 184. The great opera composer Giacomo Puccini (1858–1924) composed this charming lullaby for the infant son of one of his best friends, who had died before the baby was born. It has been a successful recital piece, recorded by major artists like Licia Albanese and Renata Tebaldi, and it can also be sung appropriately by male singers.

Source: First edition. Ricordi, Milan, 1899. Key: D.

**"The Sky Above the Roof,"** page 187. Ralph Vaughan Williams (1872–1958) based his style on scales and rhythms found in English folk songs. The poem is translated from *"Le ciel est, par-dessus le toit,"* written by Paul Verlaine (1844–1896) while he was in prison for attempted murder.

**"At the River,"** page 190, is based on a Baptist gospel song by Robert R. Lowry (1826–1899), who wrote both the tune and the text. The imagery comes from visions of the afterlife found in the Book of Revelations.

Charles Edward Ives (Danbury, CT, 1874; New York City, 1954) played the organ in several churches from his teen years on. He studied music at Yale, but he went into the life insurance field and wrote music outside of office hours. Encouraged by his wife, Harmony, Ives made remarkable musical innovations, including use of several keys at once and novel ways of forming chords. His stressful life led to a heart attack in 1918. During recuperation Ives "cleaned house" by making final copies of music written earlier, and he published *114 Songs* at his own expense in 1922. He lived long enough to see a growing acceptance of his music, which is now played often by major symphony orchestras.

Why are the chords in the accompaniment so strange? Ives knew that there are beautiful sounds that lie beyond the realm of conventional major and minor chords, and he used them to suggest ideas and feelings that are beyond our ability to know rationally or to put into words. Ives often borrowed from well-known hymns because he respected people's feelings about them. "At the River" uses some phrases of Lowry's gospel song but floats the melody over chords that contain many notes from other keys with an unearthly effect. Ives departs from Lowry's melody in measures 11–13 and again from measure 20 to the end in order to have more freedom to suggest "the throne of God." The end of the song is an unanswered question. Ives himself added the note: "The piano part must not be played heavily."

Source: "At the River," (1916), based on *Sonata No. 4, Children's Day at the Camp Meeting,* for violin and piano (1914–1915). Published in *114 Songs*.

**"By the Sea,"** page 193. Roger Quilter (1877–1953) wrote both words and music of this song when he was in his early twenties.

Source: *Three Songs of the Sea.* Forsyth, London, 1911.

"**To a Brown Girl, Dead,**" pages 196 and 198, presents a poignant picture of Harlem life. We do not know how the girl died, only that her mother has sacrificed to make her pretty. Countee Cullen (1903–1946) was a lyric poet, a leader of the Harlem Renaissance. The poem comes from his book *Color,* 1925. Margaret Bonds (Chicago, 1913; Los Angeles, 1972) was a versatile musician and a prolific composer who collaborated with Langston Hughes on stage productions.

## Musical theater songs and popular song classics

When a Broadway musical is developed, it usually goes through a long process in which songs are written and tried out, some of them rewritten or discarded. Songs may be added, revised, or dropped both before and after the show opens.

The original orchestrations of most early musicals have been lost because no one thought that future generations would want them. Published sheet music of older songs may be quite different from the version that was done onstage. In order to reach a broad market of musical amateurs, publishers often chose a "sheet-music key" so that the highest note of a song would be on the top line or space of the treble clef, regardless of how the song was sung in the show. They would also double every melody note in the piano part, even though this often does not result in a good sound. Sheet-music keys were usually used in books of "selections" from musicals. Unfortunately, the sheet music version is all we have of most older songs.

When the complete score of a musical is published, the keys and ranges of songs usually correspond to the onstage performance, and the same is true of selections from more recent musicals. If you want to audition for a musical, it may be important to find out exactly what vocal range is needed for the part you want to play.

"**Ain't Misbehavin',**" page 200, was part of an African-American night club review that was adapted for Broadway as *Hot Chocolates* (1929, 219 performances). The hit song never went out of style; its title was used for another Broadway review devoted to the music of Thomas "Fats" Waller, *Ain't Misbehavin'* (1978, 1,604 performances). Singing stars have performed this song in many different ways, but the original tempo was "slowly." Do not sing the eighth-notes evenly; "swing" them, making the onbeat eighth-notes about twice as long as the offbeat ones. The effect sounds as if the song were written in 12/8 time.

Source: original edition, piano score by Harold Potter.

"**Love Is Here to Stay,**" pages 204 and 208. When George Gershwin (1898–1937) died, he was working on songs for a film, *The Goldwyn Follies* (1938). Normally, words are written before music, but in this case Gershwin wrote the melody without having any words in mind for it. His brother Ira added these words later. Kenny Baker sang the song in the film.

"**A Cockeyed Optimist,**" page 212, from *South Pacific* (1949, 1,925 performances) occurs in the first scene, when Ensign Nellie Forbush, a U.S. Navy nurse in World War II, expresses her philosophy of life to a French civilian, Emile DeBecque. Mary Martin created the role of Nellie. Notice some unusual lines: "When the sky is . . . canary yellow"; "But every whippoorwill is selling me a bill . . ." (a play on "sold a bill of goods"); ". . . life is just a bowl of jello . . ." (a play on "life is just a bowl of cherries"). Nellie seems to have a flair for unusual combinations of ordinary words! The musical is based on James Michener's *Tales of the South Pacific.* Original key: F.

"**One Hand, One Heart,**" pages 216 and 218, from *West Side Story* (1957, 732 performances). A great conductor and composer of classical music, Leonard Bernstein (1918–1990) wrote this modern version of the Romeo and Juliet story. These wedding vows are sung by the young lovers, Maria (Carol Lawrence) and Tony (Larry Kert), in a bridal shop after closing time. Original key: G♭.

"**I'll Know,**" page 220, from *Guys and Dolls* (1950, 1,200 performances). Based on stories by Damon Runyon, this show portrays a battle of wits between New York gangsters and Salvation Army officers. This song is sung by one of the latter, Miss Sarah Brown (Isabel Bigley on stage and Jean Simmons in the film).

**"Soon It's Gonna Rain,"** page 223, from *The Fantasticks* (1960, over 12,000 performances and still running as this is written). Fans who saw this show on a date now bring their grandchildren to see it in the same tiny theater in Greenwich Village. This song is a duet between the young lovers, Luisa and Matt. Original key: C.

**"Make Someone Happy,"** page 228, from *Do-Re-Mi* (1960, 400 performances). The show is a satire on the music business and the way hit songs are created. This hit was first sung by John Reardon. Original key: E♭.

**"Far From the Home I Love,"** page 231, from *Fiddler on the Roof* (1964, 3,242 performances), is sung by Hodel, the second daughter of Tevye, a milkman. The scene is a Jewish village in Czarist Russia around 1905. Hodel is leaving home to follow Perchik, a rebellious student who has been arrested and sent into exile in Siberia. The musical is based on stories by Sholom Aleichem. Notice the flatted second scale tone, typical of Jewish folk music. Original key: C minor.

**"Yesterday,"** page 234, comes from the Beatles album *Help!* (1965). Although John Lennon's name appears by contractual agreement, Paul McCartney actually wrote both lyrics and music together in one sitting. George Martin's arrangement of the accompaniment used guitar and string quartet, an innovation for pop music. Original key: F.

**"Happiness,"** page 237, from *You're a Good Man, Charlie Brown* (1967, 1,597 performances). Based on the *Peanuts* comic strip, this show was released as a record before it was staged.

**"Anyone Can Whistle,"** pages 240 and 243, is the title song of *Anyone Can Whistle* (1964, 9 performances). Sung by Lee Remick in the first production, it has been revived as part of various reviews devoted to the music of Stephen Sondheim. Original key.

**"Believe in Yourself,"** page 246, from *The Wiz* (1975, 1,672 performances). Based on the story and characters found in L. Frank Baum's *The Wizard of Oz*, this musical had an all African-American cast. It was made into a successful motion picture. In the final scene Dorothy, played by Diana Ross, sings this song to Scarecrow, Tin Woodman, and Lion. The whole song is sung again, with some altered words, by Glenda the Good, sung by Lena Horne. Both stars sing the song in B♭ Major, beginning on F below middle C. The sheet music key is F Major, beginning on middle C.

**"What I Did for Love,"** page 250, from *A Chorus Line* (1975, 6,137 performances) is sung by Diana Morales, who is auditioning to be in the chorus of a musical. When one of the dancers injures himself, perhaps ending his career, the director asks the other auditioners how they would feel if their careers ended suddenly. Morales (first sung by Priscilla Lopez) answers with this song about her love of dancing. Original key: A♭.

**"The Greatest Love of All,"** page 254, is inseparably linked with the name of Whitney Houston. The sheet music key is a half step lower, in A Major.

**"All I Ask of You,"** page 258, from *Phantom of the Opera* (1988, over 2,650 performances). This is a duet for Christine and Raoul, shortened here to be sung by a solo voice.

# B The International Phonetic Alphabet

These are the symbols of the International Phonetic Alphabet (IPA) as they are used in singing English. They are given in this order: vowels, semivowels, consonants. You can learn more about their use in chapters 6 and 7 and about diphthongs in chapter 8.

**Vowels:**

| | | | |
|---|---|---|---|
| 1. | [i] | Ee | we, meet, key, sea, receive |
| 2. | [ɪ] | Short I | with, gym, lily, listen |
| 3. | [e] | Pure Ay | chaotic, dictates |
| 4. | [ɛ] | Open Eh | enter, merry, many, friend |
| 5. | [æ] | Short A | at, stab, act, shadow, magic |
| 6. | [a] | Bright Ah | aisle (substitute #5 or #7) |
| 7. | [ɑ] | Dark Ah | far, dark, calm, palm |
| 8. | [ɒ] | Short O | god, long (substitute #7) |
| 9. | [ɔ] | Open O | chord, author, awe, shawl |
| 10. | [o] | Pure Oh | hotel, obey |
| 11. | [ʊ] | Short U | bush, foot, wolf, look |
| 12. | [u] | Oo | flute, queue, noon, do, you |
| 13. | [ʌ] | Uh | sung, up, son, come |
| 14. | [ə] | Schwa | (2nd syl. of:) even, sofa, little |
| 15. | [ɜ] | Er | learn, her, bird, journey, myrrh |

**Semivowels:**

| | | | |
|---|---|---|---|
| 16. | [j] | Yah | yam, union, eulogy, pew, due |
| 17. | [w] | Wah | was, witch, waste, once |

**Consonants:**

| | | | |
|---|---|---|---|
| 18. | [m] | Em | sum, ma'am, dimmer, hymn |
| 19. | [n] | En | nun, liner |
| 20. | [ŋ] | Ing | sang, king, hunger, English |
| 21. | [l] | El | love, wilt, Sally |
| 22. | [r] | Ahr | red, earring, hear |
| 23. | [h] | Aitch | house, hunk, Minnehaha |
| 24. | [hw] | Which | why, whether, whiz |
| 25. | [f] | Eff | far, feel, philosophy |
| 26. | [v] | Vee | very, overt, quiver |
| 27. | [θ] | Theta | thick, thistle, cloth |
| 28. | [ð] | Edh | these, other, within, lathe |
| 29. | [s] | Ess | sat, psalm, lets, decent |
| 30. | [z] | Zee | zoom, buzzard, was, zest |
| 31. | [ʃ] | Shah | shoe, negotiate, sugar, cash |
| 32. | [ʒ] | Zsa-Zsa | leisure, garage, casual |
| 33. | [p] | Pee | pay, caper, sup |
| 34. | [b] | Bee | boy, saber, rub |
| 35. | [t] | Tee | tent, ptomaine, slat |
| 36. | [d] | Dee | die, leader, bed |
| 37. | [k] | Kay | coal, choir, technique, anchor |
| 38. | [g] | Hard Gee | girl, bigger, bug |
| 39. | [ʧ] | Cha-Cha | cello, rich, catcher |
| 40. | [ʤ] | Soft Gee | jet, jasmine, ajar, huge |

**Diphthongs:**

| | | | |
|---|---|---|---|
| 4 + 2. | [ɛɪ] | Long Ay | wave, wait, weigh, way |
| 6 + 2. | [aɪ] | Long I | life, pie, cry, aisle, Einstein |
| 9 + 2. | [ɔɪ] | Oy | boy, choice |
| 6 + 11. | [aʊ] | Ow | wow, ouch |
| 10 + 11. | [oʊ] | Long Oh | social, sew, blow, groan |
| 2 + 14. | [ɪɚ] | Ear-Diphthong | cheer, fear, mere, we're |
| 4 + 14. | [ɛɚ] | Air-Diphthong | care, hair, wear, they're |
| 7 + 14. | [ɑɚ] | Are-Diphthong | car, hearth, armor |
| 9 + 14. | [ɔɚ] | Or-Diphthong | lord, pour, your, o'er |
| 11 + 14. | [ʊɚ] | Tour-Diphthong | sure, moor, your |
| 6 + 2 + 14. | [aɪɚ] | Ire-Triphthong | fire, briar, lyre, choir |
| 6 + 11 + 14. | [aʊɚ] | Our-Triphthong | cower, sour |

# C Foreign Language Song Texts

Through singing you re-live experiences that people of other lands have expressed in their songs. You may do this by singing good English translations and sensing the national flavor of the music or by singing in the original language if you have some background in it.

The information given here does not provide a complete course in foreign language diction because that is not an appropriate goal for the first year of voice study. Your highest priority now is to improve your singing, as to sound and technique. If singing in a foreign language causes a problem and distracts you from singing well, it is better to sing a translation or a different song.

Your first need is to understand the text completely, whatever language it is. There are three possible kinds of song translations:

(1) Some songs have *singable* English translations, but the meaning of the English version is always somewhat different from the original because of the need for rhythm and rhyme;

(2) This book gives *literal* translations at the foot of the music pages, using normal English word order;

(3) *Word by word* translations, such as are given on the following pages, show exactly what each word means even when the foreign word order results in an unnatural sounding English version.

Your next need is to pronounce the words correctly. Here you will find IPA transcriptions to help you, as well as a few comments about general characteristics of each language. Again, I want to stress that these comments do not tell all about every language—that would take many more pages. My intent is to give you the most essential information, so that if you have some background in the language and assistance from your teacher, you can perform your song correctly and confidently.

## What the singer's languages have in common

Besides English, the languages represented in this book are Italian (5 songs), German (4), Spanish (3), French (1), Hebrew (1), and Latin (1).

These languages differ in the number of vowels used, but all of them have pure vowels, that is, no vowels that have diphthong shadings such as English has in "so" and "say." Also, in all of these languages the vowels always or most often have their Latin values, the ones used in the IPA. As examples, make it a habit to say [a] when you see the letter *a* and [i] when you see the letter *i*. Whatever vowel you sing, keep the quality of it pure for as long as the vowel lasts. Except for French, all of these languages have stronger (stressed) and weaker (unstressed) syllables. Transcriptions in this book indicate stress by underlining. Underlining also shows, when two vowels are in one syllable, which one of them is more important.

## Songs in Italian

The tradition of singing comes from Italy, and many teachers prefer to have students sing in Italian before any other language. Italian is a legato language; the end of a word is nearly always connected smoothly to the beginning of the next word. The flow of connected sounds is broken only by certain double consonants.

Italian vowels, not consonants, convey the energy and emotion of the language; the consonants are mostly soft, barely audible. Every stressed vowel followed by a single consonant is long, for example, *cane* [ka:ne].

Italian spelling often resembles IPA symbols, but there are some pitfalls. The letters *e* and *o* each have two pronunciations, closed and open, in stressed syllables, and the spelling does not indicate which one to use. Every *e* or *o* in a stressed syllable must be checked with a dictionary. (In unstressed syllables they are always closed.)

Consonants are gentle in Italian. [p, t, k] have no aspiration (explosiveness). [d, n, t, l] are all pronounced with the tongue lightly touching the upper teeth (dentalized).

Italian double consonants are audibly different from single ones. If possible, the consonant sound continues for at least three times as long as it takes to say a single consonant, shown in IPA this way [m:m, s:s, b:b]. When the doubled consonant is a voiceless stop, there is silence between the closing and reopening of the consonant, for example, *attacca* [at:tak:ka]. This is an exception to the legato rule.

*R* is pronounced with a single flip of the tongue-tip [ɾ] when it occurs between two vowels, otherwise it is vigorously rolled [r].

**New IPA symbols for Italian:**

| | | |
|---|---|---|
| [ː] | Lengthener | means "hold the position of the previous vowel or consonant." |
| [ɾ] | Flipped R | caro [kaɾo], morire [moɾiɾe] |

"Dolce scherza," G. A. Perti, pages 136 and 138.

doltʃe  skɛrtsa e  doltʃe  riːde
Dolce  scherza e  dolce  ride
Sweetly jests   and sweetly laughs

vaːgo labːbro e  spiːɾa  amoːr
Vago labbro e  spira  amor.
lovely lip   and breathes love.

ma talːlɛtːta   e  pɔi tutːtʃiːde
Ma t'alletta   e  poi t'uccide;
But you-it-cheers and then you-kills;

kozi afːflidːʤe kwesto kɔr
Così affligge  questo cor.
thus it-harms this  heart

"Vado ben spesso," Giovanni Bononcini, pages 140 and 143.
            [ʤovanːni bononʧiːni]

vaːdo bɛn  spesːso kandʒando lɔko
Vado ben  spesso cangiando loco,
I-go indeed often,  changing  place,

ma non sɔ    mai kandʒar deziːo
Ma non so    mai cangiar desio.
but not I-know-how ever to-change desire.

sɛmpre listesːso saɾa  il  mio fɔːko
Sempre l'istesso sarà  il  mio foco
Always the-same will-be the my fire

e  saɾɔ  sɛmpre aŋkiːo
E  sarò  sempre anch'io.
and will-be  always also-I.

"Nel cor più non mi sento," Giovanni Paisiello, page 153.
[ʤovanːni paizjɛlːlo]

nel    kɔr    pju    non mi    sɛnto
Nel    cor    più    non mi    sento
In-the heart  more   not myself I-feel

brilːlaːr la    ʤoventuː
Brillar   la    gioventù:
shine     the   youth;

kaʤoːn del    mio tormɛnto
Cagion del    mio tormento,
cause  of-the my torture,

amoːr, sɛi kolpa tu
Amor,  sei colpa tu.
Love,  are guilty you.

mi stutːsiki    mi mastiki
Mi stuzzichi,   mi mastichi,
Me you-pick-at, me you-bite,

mi punʤiki   mi pitːsiki
Mi pungichi,  mi pizzichi;
me you-prick, me you-pinch—

ke    kɔːzaɛ kwɛsta oimɛ
Che   cosa è questa, oimè!
what thing is this,    alas!

pjeta pjeta pjeta
Pietà, pietà, pietà!
Pity,  pity,  pity!

amoːrɛun ʧɛrto      ke
Amore è un certo     che,
Love  is a certain-thing that,

ke   deliraːr mi fa
Che delirar   mi fa.
that to-rave  me makes.

2. ti   sɛnto si  ti   sɛnto
   Ti   sento, si,  ti   sento,
   You I-hear, yes, you I-hear,

bɛl      fjoːr di ʤoventuː
Bel      fior  di gioventù: . . .
beautiful flower of youth, . . .

aːnima mia    sɛi tu
Anima mia,    sei tu. . . .
soul   mine, are you. . . .

kwel viːzoaun ʧɛrto         ke
Quel viso ha un certo        che . . .
That face has a  certain-something that . . .

"Santa Lucia," Teodoro Cottrau, pages 180 and 182.
[teodɔro kotːtrau]

sul     maːre lutːʧika lastro darʤɛnto
Sul     mare luccica l'astro d'argento,
On-the sea   shines  the-star of-silver;

plaːʧida ɛ londa   prɔspero ɛ il vɛnto
Placida è l'onda, prospero è il vento.
calm    is the-sea, favorable is the wind.

venite al:la:ʤile        barket:ta mia   santa luʧia
Venite all'agile         barchetta mia!  Santa Lucia!
Come  to-the-graceful little-boat mine! St.    Lucia!

kon   kwesto ʤef:firo kozi soa:ve
Con  questo zeffiro    così soave,
With this     breeze    so    gentle,

o: ko:mɛ   bɛl:lo     sta:r sul:la na:ve
O com'è     bello      star sulla  nave!
O how-it-is beautiful to-be on-the ship!

su: pas:sad:ʤɛri venite via
Su  passaggieri, venite via! Santa Lucia!
Up, passengers! come  away!

"E l'uccellino," Giacomo Puccini, page 184.
          [ʤakomo put:ʧini]

e     lut:ʧel:lino  kanta sul:la  fronda
E     l'uccellino    canta sulla   fronda:
And the-little-bird sings on-the leafy-branch:

dormi traŋkwil:lo bok:kut:ʧa damore
Dormi tranquillo, boccuccia    d'amore;
sleep   peacefully, dear-mouth of-love;

pjɛgala ʤu    kwɛl:la testina       bjonda
Piegala giù,    quella testina       bionda,
bend-it down, that      little-head  fair,

del:la tua    mam:ma pɔzala sul     kwɔre
Della tua     mamma posala sul      cuore.
of     your mama,   put-it on-the heart.
(put your head on your mama's heart.)

e     lut:ʧel:lino  kanta su kwɛl ramo
E     l'uccellino    canta su quel ramo,
And the-little-bird sings on that  branch;

tante    kozine   bɛl:le   imparerai
Tante    cosine   belle    imparerai,
so-many dear-things beautiful you-will-learn,

ma se vor:rai   konoʃ:ʃer kwantio     tamo
Ma se vorrai      conoscer quant'io      t'amo,
but if  you-want to-know  how-much-I you-love,

nes:suno al mondo potra dirlo  mai
Nessuno al mondo potrà dirlo  mai!
no-one   on earth   could say-it ever!

e     lut:ʧel:lino  kantal      ʧɛl sereno
E     l'uccellino    canta al     ciel sereno:
And the-little-bird sings to-the sky peaceful:

dormi tezɔro  mio   kwi sul mio seno
Dormi tesoro   mio   qui sul mio seno.
sleep, treasure mine, here on my  bosom.

# Songs in Spanish

Spanish is more legato than English, and the vowels carry the expressive message, just as in Italian. Spanish has many dialects, all of which use the same five vowel sounds. Spanish [i o u] are all pronounced a little more open than in Italian. Spanish [e] is much more open than Italian [e].

For the most part Spanish consonants are even softer than Italian consonants. There is no burst of air (aspiration) on plosive consonants [p, k, t]. The letters *b, c, d, g, s, v,* and *z* all vary in pronunciation according to their locations. The sounds [d, t] are dental sounds, pronounced with the tongue tip touching the teeth.

*R* may be either flipped [ɾ] or rolled [r]. In the Latin American texts found here *ll* is [ʝ].

**New IPA symbols for Spanish:**

| | | |
|---|---|---|
| [ɲ] | Enya | señor [seɲor], cariño [kariɲo]. Enya resembles [nj] but is made with the tongue tip down. |
| [x] | Ach | jota [xota], bajando [baxando]. Ach is voiceless, using friction of air between the back of the tongue and the soft palate. |
| [ɣ] | Agua | me gustan [meɣustan]. Agua is a voiced form of Ach. |
| [β] | Buzz | abierto [aβjerto], ave [aβe]. Buzz is voiced and uses air passing between both lips. |
| [ʝ] | Alla | calle [kaʝe], cuyo [kuʝo], hoy es [oʝes]. A fricative consonant, formed with the tip of the tongue against the lower front teeth and gums, using friction of air between the hump of the tongue and the hard palate. |

"De colores," page 82.

```
de   kolores se        βisten los kampos en la  primaβera
De   colores se        visten los campos en la  primavera,
With colors themselves dress the fields    in the spring,

      son los paxariʝos ke  βjenen de    fwera
. . . son los pajarillos  que vienen de    fuera,
      are the little-birds that come  from far-away,

      es el arkoiɾis ke  βemos lusir
. . . es el  arcoiris que  vemos lucir,
      is the rainbow that we-see shining,

i    por eso los gɾandes amores de mutʃos kolores
Y    por eso los grandes amores de muchos colores
and for this the great    loves    of many    colors

me ɣustan       a mi
Me gustan       a mi.
-    are pleasing to me.
```

"Cielito lindo," pages 92 and 94.

```
de    la sjeɾa         moɾena βjenen baxando
De    la Sierra        Morena vienen bajando
From the Mountains Brown  come    descending

un paɾ deoxitos      negɾos sjelito     lindo  ðe kontɾaβando
Un par de ojitos     negros, cielito    lindo, de contrabando.
a    pair of dear-eyes dark,  dear-Heaven lovely, of contraband.

ai  kanta i   no joɾes
Ay, canta y    no llores,
Ah, sing  and not weep,

poɾke  kantando se alegɾan    los koɾasones
Porque cantando se alegran    los corazones.
because singing   -   are-happy, the hearts.

paxaɾo keaβandona   su primeɾ niðo
Pajaro que abandona su primer nido
Bird    that leaves  its first   nest

reɣɾesa i  ja no         enkwentɾa   el bjen  perðiðo
Regresa y  ya no         encuentra . . . el bien  perdido.
returns and now doesn't meet          the darling lost.
```

```
ese  lunar ke  tjenes       xuntoa la  βoka
Ese  lunar que tienes . . . junto a la  boca
That mole  that you-have,  next  to the mouth,
```

```
no    se lo ðes  a  naðje        kea        mi me toka
No    se lo des  a  nadie . . .  que       a mi me toca.
don't -  it give to anyone       because [idiom: it's mine].
```

"El Tecolote," page 114.

```
tekolote ðe    gwaðjana paxaro madruɤaðor
Tecolote de    Guadiana, pajaro  madrugador,
Owl      from Guadiana, bird     early-riser;
```

```
para ke  βwelas de notʃe  ai tenjendo por suxo     el dia
Para que vuelas de noche, ay teniendo por sujo      el dia?
Why (-)  you-fly at night, oh, keeping  for yourself the day?
```

```
pobresito tekolote ja      se   kansa ðe ɤolar
Pobrecito tecolote ya      se   cansa de volar.
poor-little owl         already itself tires  of flying.
```

## Songs in French

French pronunciation is not more difficult than that of other languages in this book, but the spelling is. French spelling is as difficult for French speakers as English spelling is for us.

Pronounce all French syllables evenly, without strong stresses. Because of the smooth legato of sung French, we transcribe each syllable as a separate unit; the syllables are not grouped together into words, but into phrases.

Native French speakers pronounce most vowels with the soft palate lifted so high that no air enters the nose and no nasal resonance occurs. The exceptions to this habit are four nasalized vowels that are produced with a lowered soft palate, allowing more breath to flow through the nose than through the mouth. The distinction between oral vowels and nasalized vowels is characteristic of French.

French also uses mixed vowels (which are not diphthongs). To form mixed vowels, the lips round while the tongue *simultaneously* rises forward. (In English, when the lips round, the tongue pulls back automatically.) Two such vowels occur in our song: [y], called Ee-Oo, is made by raising the tongue as if for [i] and rounding the lips for [u]; and [œ], called Open E-O, the tongue rises as if for [ɛ] and the lips round for [ɔ].

Besides [j] and [w], French has one more semivowel, [ɥ], made by starting from [y] and gliding to the following vowel sound. In the word "nuit" [nɥi], the tongue remains lifted, but the lips lose their rounding, changing the vowel sound from [y] to [i].

If you have studied spoken French, you will notice two main differences in sung French: "mute e" is pronounced as [ə]; and the "French," uvular [ʀ] is replaced with a flipped or rolled [r].

**New IPA symbols for French:**

| | | |
|---|---|---|
| [ɑ̃] | Nasalized Ah | an [ɑ̃], enfant ɑ̃fɑ̃ |
| [ɛ̃] | Nasalized Eh | hein [ɛ̃], point [pwɛ̃] |
| [õ] | Nasalized Oh | on [õ], sont [sõ] |
| [œ̃] | Nasalized Open E-O | un [œ̃] |
| [y] | Ee-Oo | du [dy] |
| [œ] | Open E-O | fleur [flœr], leur [lœr] |
| [ɥ] | Ee-Oo Glide | nuit [nɥi] |

"Auprès de ma blonde," page 90.

1. o      ʒa rdɛ̃  də mõ  pɛ rə
   Au    jardin  de mon père
   At-the garden of my  father

le  lɔ rje    sõ  flœ ri
Les  lauriers sont fleuri,
the  laurels  are  flowered;

tu   lɛ  zwa zo  dy    mõ də
Tous les  oiseaux du    monde
all   the  birds    of-the world

võ   ti   fɛ rə  lœ   rni
Vont y    faire  leur nids . . .
go    and make their nests . . .

2. la    kaj    la  tu rtə rɛ lə
   La   caill', la  tourterelle
   The  quail,  the  turtledove,

e    lə  ʒɔli    pɛ rdri
Et   le  joli     perdrix,
and  the pretty partridge

e    la  blɑ̃ʃə   kɔlõ bə
Et   la  blanche colombe,
and  the white    dove,

ki    ʃɑ̃ tə   ʒu  re   nɥi
Qui  chante jour et    nuit
who  sings  day  and night . . .

3. ɛl   ʃɑ̃ tə   pu    rlɛ fi jə
   Ell'  chante pour  les filles
   She sings  for     the girls

ki    nõ       pwɛ̃  də ma ri
Qui  n'ont     point de mari;
who  not-have any   of husband;

sɛ     pɑ pu    rmwa kɛl    ʃɑ̃ tə
C'est pas pour moi   qu'ell'  chante,
it-is  not for   me      that-she sings,

kar   ʒɑ̃      ne   œ  ʒɔ li
Car   j'en     ai   un joli.
because I-of-them have a  pretty (one).

Refrain: oprɛ    də ma blõ də
         Auprès de ma blonde
         Close   to  my blonde (wife)

kil    fɛ   bõ   dɔr mir
Qu'il  fait  bon  dormir!
how-it does good to-sleep!

## Songs in German

German and English come from the same roots and are both classed as Germanic languages. Characteristics of Germanic languages include strong syllabic stress, energetic consonants, nonlegato articulation, and aspiration (breathiness) of sounds such as [h], [p], [t], and [k].

A significant feature of German is vowel length: compare "satt" [zat], which has a short vowel, with "Saat" [zaːt], which has a long one. Precise time studies of speech have shown that even in rapid conversation a native German takes more time to say a long vowel than a short one. If a short vowel occurs in singing a note, the following consonant takes up part of the rhythmic value. A long vowel, shown by a lengthener [ː], is stretched to fill as much of the note value as possible.

German uses the two mixed vowels described for French, plus two more: Short I-U, with the tongue lifted for [ɪ] and the lips rounded for [ʊ], and Long Ay-Oh, with the tongue lifted for [e] and lips rounded for [o].

Typical of German are the two sounds of "ch." Form your mouth to say [ɪ], then make a soft noise by blowing air through the opening; the resulting sound is [ç], which Germans call the "Ich sound." Next form your mouth to say [a], then make a soft noise by blowing through the opening; the sound is [x], called the "Ach sound." The difference between "Ich" and "Ach" occurs automatically as a result of the preceding sound; there is little chance of saying the wrong one. Keep these sounds light and soft, not exaggerated.

The German "r" has varied forms, somewhat subject to personal taste. Avoid the American [r]; use flipped [ɾ] and tongue-rolled [r], more or less as in Italian. Uvular [ʀ], heard in German speech, is not used in artistic singing.

### IPA symbols needed for German:

| | | |
|---|---|---|
| [y] | Ee-Oo | Güte [gy:tə], über [y:bər] |
| [ʏ] | Short I-U | entrückt [ɛntrʏkt] |
| [ø] | Ay-Oh | krönst [krø:nst], |
| [œ] | Open E-O | Schöpfer [ʃœ pfər] |
| [ç] | Ich sound | reicht [raeçt], ewig [e:vɪç] |
| [x] | Ach sound | Hauch [haox], Baches [baxəs] |

"Bitten," Ludwig van Beethoven, pages 156 and 158.
[bɪt:tən lu:tvɪç fan be:tho:fən]

got   daenə gy:tə      raeçt   zo: vaet
Gott, deine Güte       reicht  so  weit,
God, your  goodness reaches as  far

zo vaet      di: vɔlkən ge:ən
So weit      die Wolken gehen,
as far [as] the clouds  go.

du: krø:nst ʊns mɪt  barmhɛrtsɪçkaet
Du  krönst  uns mit  Barmherzigkeit,
You crown   us  with compassion

ʊnt aelst  ʊns baetsuʃte:ən
Und eilst, uns beizustehen.
and hurry us   by-to-stand.

hɛr   maenə bʊrk    maen fɛls maen hɔrt
Herr, meine Burg,   mein Fels, mein Hort,
Lord, my    fortress, my   rock, my  protection,

fɛrnɪm  maen fle:n,     mɛrk laof maen vɔrt
Vernimm mein Flehn,     merk' auf mein Wort,
Hear    my   pleading, notice   my   word,

dɛn  ɪç vɪl  fo:r  di:r be:tən
Denn ich will vor   dir beten!
for  I   want before you to-pray.

"An die Musik," Franz Schubert, pages 160 and 162.
[an di: muzi:k, frants ʃu:bərt]

du: hɔldə kʊnst ɪn vi:fi:l     graoən ʃtʊnden
Du  holde Kunst, in wieviel     grauen Stunden,
You lovely art, in how-many gray    hours,

vo:   mɪç dɛs le:bəns vɪldər kraes ʊmʃtrɪkt
Wo    mich des Lebens wilder Kreis umstrickt,
where me   the life's  wild   ring  around-binds,

hast du: maen hɛrts tsu: varmər liːb lɛntːtsundən
Hast du mein Herz zu warmer Lieb' entzunden,
have you my heart to warm love kindled,

hast mɪç ɪn aenə bɛsrə vɛlt lɛntrʏkt
Hast mich in eine bessre Welt entrückt!
have-you me into a better world wafted-away!

ɔft hat laen zɔøftsər daenər harf lɛntflɔsən
Oft hat ein Seufzer, deiner Harf' entflossen,
often has a sigh, from-your harp flowed-away,

aen zyːsər haelɪgər akːkɔrt fɔn diːr,
Ein süsser, heiliger Akkord von dir
a sweet, holy chord from you,

den hɪmːməl bɛsrər tsaetən miːr lɛrʃlɔsən
Den Himmel bessrer Zeiten mir erschlossen,
the heaven of-better times to-me opened;

duː hɔldə kʊnst lɪç daŋkə diːr dafyːr
Du holde Kunst, ich danke dir dafür!
you lovely art, I thank you for-that.

"Wanderers Nachtlied," Franz Schubert, pages 164 and 165.
[vandərərs naxtliːt frants ʃuːbərt]

yːbər alːən gɪpfəln
Über allen Gipfeln
Over all mountain-peaks

ɪst ruː
Ist Ruh,
is rest,

in alːən vɪpfəln
In allen Wipfeln
in all tree-tops

ʃpyːrəst duː
Spürest du
feel you

kaom aenən haox
Kaum einen Hauch;
hardly a breath;

diː føːglaen ʃvaegən ɪm valdə
Die Vöglein schweigen im Walde
the little-birds are-silent in-the forest.

vartə nuːr baldə
Warte nur, balde
Wait only, soon

ruːəst duː laox
Ruhest du auch.
rest you also.

"Widmung," Robert Franz, pages 172 and 174.
[vɪtmuŋ roːbɛrt frants]

oː daŋkə nɪçt fyːr diːzə liːdər
O danke nicht fur diese Lieder,
O thank not for these songs,

miːr tsiːmt ɛs daŋkbar diːr tsuː zaen
Mir ziemt es dankbar dir zu sein;
to-me suits it thankful to-you to be.

duː gaːpst ziː  miːr  ɪç geːbə viːdər
Du gabst sie  mir,  ich gebe wieder
You gave  them to-me; I  give  back

vas  jɛtst ʊnt aenst ʊnt eːvɪç  daen
Was jetzt und einst und ewig  dein.
what now and  soon  and eternally yours.

daen zɪnt ziː alːə ja  gəveːzən
Dein sind sie alle ja  gewesen;
Yours have they all  indeed been;

aos  daenər liːbən aogən lɪçt
Aus  deiner lieben Augen Licht
from your  dear  eyes'  light

hap ɪc ziː  trɔølɪç apgəleːzən
Hab ich sie  treulich abgelesen:
have I  them truly  read-off:

kɛnst duː di  aegnən liːdər niçt
Kennst du  die eignen Lieder nicht?
know  you the own  songs not?


## A song in Hebrew

The "ch" sound is pronounced [x] as in German "Bach."

"Shalom Chaverim," Israeli folk song, p. 87.

ʃalom  xavɛrim  ləhitraot
Shalom chaverim lehitraot.
Peace,  friends,  till-meeting.

# D Glossary of Vocal and Musical Terms

Note: Many musical terms are Italian words, some of which are found in English dictionaries because they are so frequently used.

**Acoustics** Scientific study of sound.

**A tempo, a tempo primo** In a steady tempo, used to resume tempo after an interruption or a temporary change.

**Ad lib., ad libitum** At liberty; freely with respect to timing.

**Adam's apple** A protuberance in front of the neck formed by the thyroid cartilage.

**Agility** Ability to sing a series of quick notes rapidly.

**Allegretto** In a somewhat lively tempo, less quick than allegro.

**Allegro** In a lively tempo.

**Alto** A low female voice, especially in choral music.

**Andante** In a slow tempo, at a walking pace.

**Andantino** In a moderately slow tempo, slightly quicker than andante.

**Appoggiatura** An ornamental melodic tone, often written small.

**Aria** Air; an Italian vocal composition; an elaborate solo in an opera, cantata, or oratorio.

**Articulation** Aspect of diction, relating to consonant clarity.

**Art song** An accompanied vocal composition with artistic intent.

**Arytenoid cartilages** Two small ladle-shaped cartilages whose movement adjusts the position of the posterior end of the vocal folds.

**Aspirate** (verb) To expel with a sound of moving air; (adj.) characterized by a sound of moving air.

**Attack** (noun or verb) Beginning of a tone.

**Balanced tone** Singing production with complete coordination between the action of the vocal folds and the action of the variable resonators.

**Ballad** A narrative folk song that uses the same melody for each stanza; a gentle, expressive pop song.

**Baritone** A male voice of medium range, between tenor and bass.

**Baroque** A musical style that was current roughly from 1600 to 1750; composers include Purcell and Bach.

**Bass** The lowest male voice type; the lowest note of a chord; a low-pitched stringed instrument.

**Belt** (verb, slang) To deliver forcefully.

**Belt voice** A technique of energized singing with high laryngeal position and little sensation of escaping air (source: Jo Estill, NATS master class, 1985).

**Blended register** A series of notes of medium pitch that have some qualities of light registration and some of heavy registration.

**Breath control, breath management** The art and skill of supplying the right amount of air at the right degree of pressure to perform music artistically.

**Breathy tone** An inefficient vocal tone accompanied by the sound of escaping air, caused by incomplete closure of the vocal folds during tone production.

**Bridge** The point at which the singer is aware of passing from one vocal register to another.

**Calando** Simultaneously becoming slower and softer.

**Cantabile** In a lyric, legato singing style.

**Cantata** A vocal composition for solo and/or chorus, usually in several sections called movements.

**Catch breath** A quick, partial refilling of the lungs.

**Change of voice** The lowering of a teenager's voice during puberty, caused by the growth of the larynx and the vocal folds.

**Chest** Thorax—the section of the body enclosed by the ribs, breastbone, upper spine, and diaphragm.

**Chest register** Chest voice, heavy register, notes of the lower range made with thick vocal folds; the usual speech range of men and most women (so called because of detectable vibrations in the rib cage).

**Chord** Two or more notes sounded simultaneously.

**Chorus** Choir; refrain or recurring portion of a song.

**Classical** A musical style that was current from roughly 1750 to 1825; composers include Paisiello and early Beethoven.

**Clavicular breathing** Breathing by raising and lowering the chest, as exhausted athletes do when they need to exchange large quantities of air without concern for control (named after the collarbone, or clavicle).

**Colla voce** With the voice—an instruction to the accompanist that the singer needs rhythmic freedom at a certain point.

**Con anima** With soul, with spirit.

**Con espress., con espressione** With expression.

**Con moto** With motion, moving along.

**Con spirito** With spirit, spiritedly.

**Consonants** Speech sounds produced with partial or complete stoppage of breath flow.

**Continuants** Consonant sounds capable of being prolonged.

**Contralto** The term used in opera or concert music for a low female voice.

**Cresc., crescendo** Getting louder.

**Cricoid cartilage** A ring-shaped cartilage at the top of the windpipe, the basis of the larynx.

**Crooning** A casual style of singing pop songs with a microphone.

**Da capo al fine, D. C.** Literally, from the head to the end, i.e., return to the beginning and sing it over again to the point where the word *fine* occurs.

**Diaphragm** A large dome-shaped muscular membrane that separates the chest from the abdominal cavity, active in inhalation.

**Diaphragmatic-costal breathing** A method of breath management that employs expansion and muscular action in the lower ribs, waist area, and abdomen externally and the diaphragm internally.

**Diction** Formation and delivery of the words of vocal music.

**Dim. e rit., diminuendo e ritardando** Getting softer and slower.

**Diphthong** Combination of two vowel sounds in one syllable.

**Dolce, dolce e carezzevole** Sweetly, sweetly and caressingly.

**Duet** A musical composition for two performers.

**Dynamics** Degrees of loudness and softness.

**Enunciation** An aspect of diction concerned with production and clarity of vowels and syllables.

**Epigastrium** The upper area of the abdomen, above the waist and below the ribs.

**Epiglottis** Leaf-shaped cartilage that lowers to cover the larynx during swallowing.

**Exhalation** Expiration, breathing out.

**Expression** The act of making feelings and thoughts known to others.

**Falsetto** A light, high register of the male voice made with thin vocal folds.

**False vocal folds** Two projecting muscular structures lying just above the "true" vocal folds and parallel to them.

**Fine** End.

**Flexibility** Ability of the voice to sing with agility and to produce sudden changes in pitch, dynamics, and quality.

**Focus** A sense of concentrated vibratory energy.

**Folk song** A song that is widely known, transmitted chiefly from person to person without being written down. The original composer may or may not be known. A folk song is normally performed with an improvised accompaniment (one not precisely written out in musical notation) or with no accompaniment, except for artistic arrangements made by someone other than the originator of the song. The latter case describes the songs included here as "Traditional Songs."

**Forcing** Singing with unnecessary muscular effort that interferes with the desired actions of singing.

**Free tone** An unrestrained, spontaneously produced sound without any evidence of rigid tension.

**Frequency** Rate of vibrations (cycles) per second, expressed in Hertz; e.g., A above middle C vibrates at a frequency of 440 Hz.

**Fundamental** The basic tone produced by the whole of a vibrating mass, having a lower frequency than any of the overtones.

**Glottal attack** Onset of a tone produced by blowing the closed vocal folds apart with a sharp, coughlike sound.

**Glottis** The opening between the vocal folds.

**Hard palate** Bony front portion of the roof of the mouth.

**Harmony** Chords; the art of arranging chords artistically.

**Head register** Head voice, light register, higher tones of the voice, made with thin vocal folds (so called because of perceived sympathetic vibrations in the head).

**Hertz** Cycles per second (abbreviated Hz).

**Hum** To produce pitches while exhaling through the nose only.

**Hyoid bone** U-shaped bone that anchors the base of the tongue.

**Inflection** Pitch variation of the speaking voice.

**Inhalation** Inspiration, breathing in.

**Intercostal muscles** Short muscles between the ribs, active in inhalation.

**Interpretation** The art of re-creating the music imagined by a composer on the basis of written musical notation.

**Intonation** Degree of accuracy in producing pitches.

**Involuntary** Not resulting from conscious intention.

**Key** The organization of tones in relation to a keynote, also called the tonic or tonal center. The concept of key includes a perceived need for a piece of music to reach a final point of rest on the keynote.

**Largo** Broad, slow.

**Laryngoscope** An instrument invented by Manuel Garcia in 1855 for examining the larynx, consisting of a dental mirror and a focused light source.

**Larynx** Voice box—cartilaginous enclosure that surrounds the vocal folds.

**Legato** Connected, with no discernable break in sound.

**Leggiero e distintamente** Lightly and distinctly.

**Lento** Slow.

**Lied** German art song (plural, lieder).

**Lyric** Text of a pop song.

**Major scale** A scale with a major third between the first and third notes (see chapter 12).

**Melody** Tones in succession, perceived as a musical line.

**Meno mosso** Less quickly.

**Meter** The division of music into measures or bars, each with a specified number of beats.

**Mezzo-soprano** Female voice of medium range, especially in opera and concert music.

**Minor scale** A scale with a minor third between the first and third notes (see chapter 12).

**Moderato** In a medium tempo.

**Molto** Very much.

**Musical** Short for "musical play," a play with a significant number of songs.

**Nasality** A distortion of tone caused by too much air passing above a lowered soft palate and through the nose.

**Node** Nodule—a swelling on the edge of a vocal fold, caused by the natural healing process that follows overuse or irritation of the vocal folds.

**Octave** Distance between a note and the nearest note with the same name.

**Opera** A theatrical entertainment with most or all of the text sung rather than spoken.

**Oratorio** A lengthy religious work for soloists and chorus meant for concert performance (i.e., not staged).

**Overtone** A tone produced by vibration of a fraction of a vibrating body, thus a higher tone than the fundamental.

**Pharynx** Throat; the cavity behind the mouth, between the larynx and the nose.

**Phonetics** The science of speech sounds and their representation through written symbols.

**Phrase** (vocal) A series of notes sung on one breath; (musical) a series of melodic notes perceived as an expressive unit analogous to a clause or sentence in verbal language. (A musical phrase is not limited by breath capacity and may embrace several vocal phrases.)

**Phrasing** The art of shaping music expressively, including decisions as to when to breathe.

**Pitch** A property of tone, resulting from frequency of vibration, e.g., high pitch, low pitch.

**Più mosso** More motion.

**Poco** A little.

**Projection** Transmitting the text and tone from the singer to the most distant members of an audience.

**Pronunciation** An aspect of diction, including correctness of speech sounds.

**Pure vowel** A single vowel sound without diphthong coloring.

**Range** Distance between the highest and lowest note of a song or of a person's voice.

**Refrain** Part of a song that is sung more than once but always with the same words. See Verse.

**Register** A series of similar-sounding notes produced by a similar mechanism or vocal adjustment (named after a row of similar pipes on a pipe organ).

**Release** End of a tone.

**Repertoire** The list of pieces that a musician is ready to perform on short notice.

**Resonance** Intensification of a musical sound by sympathetic vibration.

**Resonators** Cavities whose size and shape cause air in them to vibrate sympathetically in response to a sound source, such as the vocal folds, strengthening and reinforcing the sound.

**Rhythm** Patterns created by the relative length, loudness, and perceived importance of notes.

**Rit., ritardando.** Slowing down.

**Rit., ritenuto.** Suddenly slowed down.

**Romantic** A musical style prevalent in the 1800s; composers include Beethoven (in his later compositions), Schumann, and Franz.

**Scale** A series of pitches arranged in order of frequency within an octave, most commonly seven-toned scales called major and minor.

**Soft palate** Velum—soft portion of the roof of the mouth.

**Soprano** Highest female voice; highest part in a choir.

**Sostenuto** In a sustained, legato manner.

**Staccato** Separated, not connected.

**Straight tone** A tone that lacks vibrato.

**Strophic** Constructed in stanzas, each sung to the same melody.

**Technique** "What you can do;" your ability to manage your voice consciously; exercises to increase your abilties.

**Tempo** Rate of speed in music.

**Tempo di minuetto** At the speed of a minuet, a dance in triple meter from the 1700s.

**Tenor** Highest male voice.

**Ten., tenuto** Held, slightly lengthened.

**Thorax** See Chest.

**Throat** See Pharynx.

**Through composed** Not composed in repetitive stanzas.

**Thyro-arytenoid muscles** The muscular body of the vocal folds.

**Thyroid cartilage** The largest cartilage of the larynx, forming its sides.

**Timbre** Tone quality, the distinctive character of a tone, caused by the cumulative effect of the fundamental and its overtones.

**Tone** A musical sound of a definite pitch and timbre.

**Trachea** Windpipe.

**Tremolo** (vocal) A vibrato that is faulty in being too wide, too fast, or too slow; (instrumental) rapid repetition of a tone.

**Trill** Regular, rapid alternation of a tone and its neighbor.

**Triphthong** Combination of three vowels in one syllable.

**Unvoiced consonants** Made without vocal fold vibration.

**Uvula** The small mass of flesh that hangs down from the soft palate above the tongue.

**Velum** Soft palate.

**Verse** Part of a song that prepares us to hear a refrain or chorus; the verse may give information about the character who is singing. If the verse is sung more than once, the words will change each time, but the refrain will always have the same words.

**Vibrato** Regular oscillation of a tone above and below a perceived pitch center, also slightly affecting the timbre and loudness of the tone.

**Vigoroso** Vigorously.

**Vocal folds, vocal cords** Two muscular structures formed by the thyro-arytenoid muscles, capable of closing over the windpipe and of vibrating in response to air pressure from the lungs, resulting in vocal tone.

**Vocal tract** The various organs from the lungs to the lips that collaborate to produce speech and singing.

**Voice box** Larynx.

**Voiced consonants** Made with vocal fold vibration.

**Volume** Perceived loudness of tone.

**Vowel** Speech unit (phoneme) characterized by unimpeded flow of breath.

**Whisper** Breathy speech made without vocal fold vibration (although the folds are held in contact with each other along part of their length, and for this reason whispering does not rest the vocal folds).

# Index of Persons and Song Sources

# Index of Vocal and Musical Terms

*Use this page to jot down more exercises or to begin composing your own songs!*

*Use this page to jot down more exercises or to begin composing your own songs!*